2 MINUTE ANSWER GUIDE FOR NONPROFITS

ACKNOWLEDGMENTS

The publication of this guide has been made possible through a generous grant from the S. Mark Taper Foundation. We thank the Foundation for underwriting the development and publication of this much-needed resource.

The S. Mark Taper Foundation, founded in 1989, is a private family foundation dedicated to enhancing the quality of people's lives by supporting nonprofit organizations and their work in our communities.

We would also like to thank The Carol and James Collins Foundation for funding the printing of this guide. And we would like to thank The Ahmanson Foundation for funding the development of the online version of this guide.

Finally, we thank the following individuals for contributing their time and expertise to the development of this guide: Rachel Brookhart, Mike Browning, Richard Diaz, Maura Harrington, Howard Levine, Janet Levine, Ron Milam, Patty Oertel, Carmelita Ramirez-Sanchez, William Ramseyer, Arthur Rieman, Bruce Rosen, Lewis Sharpstone, Jennifer Li Shen, Belinda Teitel, Roz Teller and Anne Whatley.

ABOUT THE PARTNERS

For 30 years, the Center for Nonprofit Management has stood as the premier resource for the Southern California nonprofit community. By providing assistance in a variety of areas, the Center has supported thousands of organizations as they meet the needs of their communities. Each year the Center serves more than 5,000 board members, staff, and executives from more than 1,000 nonprofit organizations. For more information, go to **www.cnmsocal.org.**

Cause Communications has used research, creativity and consulting to build the capacity of more than 20,000 nonprofit leaders since 1999. Part think tank, part doers, Cause's approach to accelerating social change is to distill complex ideas into easy-to-understand tools. Learn more at **www.CauseCommunications.org.**

Authors: Regina Birdsell & R. Christine Hershey
Project Writers: Sheena Daniels, Nicole Howson
Project Researcher/Advisor: Jan Kern
Copy Editor: Patty Park
Creative Direction: R. Christine Hershey
Designers: Kristin Moore, Barbara Yeh

TABLE OF CONTENTS

1   Acknowledgments
1   About the Partners

INTRODUCTION
3   New Tools for a New Nonprofit Landscape
4   How to Use this Guide

5   **CHAPTER 1:** LEADERSHIP

25   **CHAPTER 2:** LEGAL

41   **CHAPTER 3:** BOARDS AND GOVERNANCE

61   **CHAPTER 4:** FINANCE

77   **CHAPTER 5:** FUNDRAISING

95   **CHAPTER 6:** MARKETING AND COMMUNICATIONS

113 **CHAPTER 7:** STRATEGIC PLANNING

131 **CHAPTER 8:** EVALUATION

145 **CHAPTER 9:** MANAGING PEOPLE

165 **CHAPTER 10:** TECHNOLOGY AND FACILITIES

183 REFERENCES

CONTENTS

NEW TOOLS FOR A NEW NONPROFIT LANDSCAPE

Let's face it: Running a successful nonprofit is demanding. Things change constantly and it's not always easy to keep up with the latest technology trends or legal requirements when you're focused on your mission. We get it. That's why we're here.

More than a decade ago, we published The Nonprofit Answer Book. It has been widely used, but times have changed.

"Technology" for nonprofits used to mean having a fax machine. Back then, we had no idea that demand would explode when a flailing economy would reduce foundation funding while government cut social services. We anticipated that the size and complexity of our sector would grow, but we couldn't have known that corporate accounting scandals would inspire increased scrutiny and regulation for nonprofits. More than that, today's executive director must be more than a manager. To meet mission objectives, he or she must emerge as a leader who guides the organization with vision and big-picture strategy.

Yes, times have changed.

But we know one thing hasn't changed: our collective commitment to mission. Whether you address homelessness, health, poverty, the arts, education or any of the causes that make our sector so vibrant and necessary, it's passion for mission that truly defines us.

The idea for this book emerged out of conversations between the Center for Nonprofit Management and Cause Communications, a pioneer nonprofit communications organization. We jointly recognized that new tools were needed to make that passion work in today's rapidly changing landscape.

This book is the result. In developing it, we were guided by the singular objective that drives us both: to help make your nonprofit the very best it can be.

HOW TO USE THIS GUIDE

We know you're busy. That's why we've organized this guide into a user-friendly, FAQ format full of "two-minute answers."

We designed it this way so you would have ready information at your fingertips when you need it.

Each section covers an area of critical importance to effectively leading nonprofit organizations. Within each tab, you'll find quick answers to 10 of the most frequently asked questions we receive. These are weighty topics, so we've also included resources throughout the book that will help you to learn more about any given subject.

You should also know that our online version of this book (www.nonprofitanswerguide.org) is a little different, as we've included a ton of extra online resources for easy clicking. We also hope you'll take time to post your own tips and submit questions on the website.

It's our hope that this book offers practical, powerful resources and tools that will help your organization continue to affect lives and effect change.

Now let's get started. Happy reading ...

1

LEADERSHIP

It used to be that the head of an organization focused on running day-to-day operations effectively.

Bringing in the funds for programming and keeping folks happy were enough. Times have changed.

Today's executive director must manage, of course; but that's only a small part of the job. The tough part is evolving from manager to leader. It's not about hierarchy. It's about injecting your vision to advance mission throughout your organization.

This chapter looks at some of the trends and best practices in leadership. We know it's not easy, so we offer up guidance and some of the best resources we know of to help make the transition. In fact, this whole book helps to support you in this effort. Whether it's communications, fundraising or governance, we want everyone who cares about your mission to be guided by a bigger picture vision.

In the end, we know your organization will be better for it.

Q | What does an effective nonprofit leader look like?

A "A strong nonprofit leader drives a sense of mission down through the organization, upward into the board and outward in to the community. He or she is willing to do whatever it takes to enable the organization to follow their mission effectively." *(Light, P. 2002. Grasping for the Ring: Defining Strong Nonprofit Leadership)*

Sound like a tall order? It is. In fact, leadership is the starting point to effective performance, organization-wide. To successfully lead and move his or her mission forward, today's nonprofit leader needs to be more than just "the boss." Research shows that today's leader needs a comprehensive set of financial, operational and executive skills that combine the best qualities of corporate-world "C-level" executives (think CEO, CFO, COO, CMO and the like).

A great nonprofit leader is of course a "big idea" person. But he or she is also the organization's chief storyteller, brand advocate, brand guardian, crisis spokesperson, chief marketing officer and chief fundraiser. To be effective in these roles, he or she must be authentic, and be able to connect, collaborate, persuade, mediate and negotiate with the best.

A great leader is also the ambassador for the health of his or her organization, both structurally and financially. This means he or she is responsible for building and maintaining relationships that enable the organization to flourish. He or she must recruit and retain the talent, and supply the tools necessary to develop a strong infrastructure and a culture that builds morale.

A great leader is "tapped in," to his or her constituents, staff, board and the social and economic conditions that affect their mission. Faced with funding shortfalls, increased demand for services, and donors seeking demonstrated results for their dollars, today's leader is a master at adapting, recognizing challenges to be overcome and seizing opportunities as they arise. Innovation is the name of the game and a great leader is adept at making tough decisions that drive the mission forward, and keep the organization financially stable.

THE BEST LEADERS:

▸ Have strong executive, operational and financial skills.

▸ Are emotionally intelligent, trustworthy, persuasive, perceptive and flexible.

▸ Infuse the organization with a commitment to big-picture vision.

▸ Advocate for the mission at every turn.

▸ Collaborate with people and organizations that can help to advance the cause.

▸ Motivate people with a proactive attitude and a commitment to set and reach goals.

▸ Fundraise and encourage the board to do so too.

▸ Clarify board and staff relationships and encourage open communications.

▸ Embrace participation, build strong teams and encourage risk taking.

No. 1

Most of all, a great leader, leads. Everyone around you should understand where you are headed and why. Ideally, they will live for it. This is where it's your job to constantly express the mission with enthusiasm and build the big picture into absolutely everything. If it seems like it's not working, resist the urge to blame. Instead, explore the motivations and interests of employees, volunteers, stakeholders and board members. Maybe it's time to get some insights into what's driving people (or not) toward your mission.

To lead people, walk beside them...As for the best leaders, the people do not notice their existence. The next best, the people honor and praise. The next, the people fear; and the next, the people hate...When the best leader's work is done the people say, 'We did it ourselves!'

- Lao-Tsu

As a leader, it's your job to constantly express your mission with enthusiasm and build the big picture into absolutely everything.

QUICK TIP

Q What is "emotional competency" and how does it relate to effectively leading a nonprofit?

A Effective leadership is not simply about being a charismatic person. Instead, it's about gaining a specific set of skills to help you do the job right.

In fact, research has shown that effective leaders have a strong set of emotional skills in common that manifests in a variety of leadership "styles." This is where a leader becomes more than a manager. And where a nonprofit evolves from an organization doing good to an organization doing great.

These emotional competencies allow a leader the flexibility to choose an appropriate leadership style or approach, to respond fluidly to situations that arise, adapt as needed and ultimately elicit the best results.

FOUR LEADERSHIP STYLES THAT ARE MOST EFFECTIVE IN NONPROFIT SITUATIONS

The Style	Associated Phrase	How it Works
Authoritative	"Come with me."	States the goal but gives people the freedom to choose how to get there.
Democratic	"What do you think?"	Gives people a voice in decisions, builds flexibility and responsibility and generates fresh ideas.
Coaching	"Try this."	Focuses on personal development and helps people meet their goals.
Affiliative	"People come first."	Builds team harmony and morale.

Adapted from *The Six Leadership Styles at a Glance, Leadership that Gets Results,* by Daniel Goleman, *Harvard Business Review,* March-April 2000.

By emotional competency or strength, we're really talking about the ability to manage yourself and your relationships effectively. This is achieved through five fundamental capabilities:

1. **SELF-AWARENESS.** This is the ability to recognize and understand your moods, emotions and drives, as well as their effect on others. Self-aware individuals are self-confident and recognize not only their strengths but also their weaknesses.

2. **SELF-REGULATION.** This is the ability to control or redirect disruptive impulses and moods and think before you act. This results in trustworthiness and integrity, comfort with ambiguity and openness to change.

3. **MOTIVATION.** This is a passion to work for reasons that go beyond money or status and a drive to pursue goals with energy and persistence. This results in a strong drive to achieve; optimism, even in the face of failure; and organizational commitment.

4. **EMPATHY.** This is the ability to understand the emotional makeup of other people and the skill to adapt according to the reactions of others. This skill allows leaders to build and retain talent. It also results in cross-cultural sensitivity and the ability to effectively service constituents.

5. **SOCIAL SKILLS.** This is the ability to manage relationships and build networks. It's the ability to find common ground and build rapport. It allows leaders to be persuasive, build and lead teams, and drive change.

Source: *What Makes a Leader,* by Daniel Goleman, Harvard Business Review, Nov.- Dec. 1998.

It goes without saying that an effective leader needs to have vision and passion along with the analytical and technical skills necessary to master the responsibilities of the job. But emotional competence is really the key to putting it all into practice.

Getting there is possible. With study and practice, anyone can readily overcome tendencies that might negatively affect their ability to build and maintain healthy professional relationships and effectively manage situations that arise. To help facilitate your process, try practicing the skills above. Then, ask for feedback from others and adjust as you go. If you're unsure, consider approaching a leadership coach for assistance. A coach can offer objective insight to help you see yourself and situations more clearly and guide the changes you wish to make.

Q | What nonprofit functions are most in need of strengthening?

A Nonprofits are typically organized into major functional areas, such as central administration, governance and programming. To be sustainable over the long term, each functional area must operate efficiently and effectively and take its place as part of the whole.

The problem arises when cutbacks, programmatic shifts, changing funder and donor needs and the like, take the stage. In such cases, resource-strapped nonprofits are stretched too thin. As a result, less essential functions may become neglected and begin to weaken. This, in turn, affects the organization's ability to fulfill its mission.

According to a recent study by the Weingart Foundation, today's nonprofits identify the following functions as most in need of attention:

BOARD LEADERSHIP AND DEVELOPMENT. The need for a strong nonprofit board cannot be overstated. Board members connect the community with an organization's mission, vision and values. As stewards, they educate the community about the organization's work and they support the organization with resources needed to fulfill its mission. They hold the organization accountable, and provide fiscal oversight. Many nonprofits are struggling to recruit members who can help move their mission forward and, once recruited, they are unsure of how to keep boards active and participating. For tips on keeping your board engaged, see Chapter 3: Boards and Governance.

PROGRAM EVALUATION AND STRATEGIC LEARNING. Nonprofits recognize the need to regularly assess and evaluate programs and operations in order to better target their constituency, maintain morale and keep their organizations energized. Unfortunately, many of these nonprofits are simply overwhelmed keeping programs running. As a result they forgo the evaluation and learning opportunities necessary to help build a more sustainable operation. To learn about how you can easily incorporate program evaluation and strategic learning into your nonprofit, read Chapter 7: Strategic Planning and Chapter 8: Evaluation.

▶ According to a recent study commissioned by the Weingart Foundation, program evaluation and engaged board leadership topped the list among nonprofit leaders asked to prioritize their capacity building needs.

To be sustainable, each functional area of your nonprofit must take its place as part of the whole.

QUICK TIP

No. 3

HUMAN RESOURCE DEVELOPMENT. Nonprofits need to focus on leadership transition. They need to find new ways to recruit and cultivate "next generation" organizational leaders. They also need to build capacity to recruit and keep talent and supply the technical resources necessary to carry out their work. To learn about strengthening your HR function, see Chapter 9: Managing People.

FINANCIAL MANAGEMENT. Nonprofits need to build the financial capacity necessary to maintain organizational stability. And financial viability is key. A stable nonprofit is able to adapt to changing environments and more effectively serve the community. To learn about building financial capacity, read Chapter 4: Finance.

FUNDRAISING. Though nonprofits and their boards often understand the impact of fundraising in maintaining a strong, sustainable organization, they may think that bringing more dollars in the door is the single answer to their problems. As a result, they underemphasize the need to integrate fundraising with marketing and communications, board governance, evaluation, HR and financial management. In Chapter 5: Fundraising, and Chapter 6: Marketing and Communications, you'll learn more about amplifying fundraising and communications by building strong functions in every area.

HOW TO STRENGTHEN ALL OF YOUR NONPROFIT FUNCTIONS

Seek out nonprofit capacity-building services in your community. Look for nonprofit coaching and consulting services, organizational assessment services, training and workshops and more. In Southern California, visit www.cnmsocal.org to learn more.

Visit www.nonprofitanswerguide.org **for timely sector resources and more expert answers to your most immediate nonprofit questions.**

QUICK TIP

Q What is all this talk about capacity building? What areas can be addressed to build organizational capacity? How can it be integrated into the organization?

A Nonprofit capacity building refers to the activities that help an organization fulfill its mission and sustain itself. This may manifest in the development of mission-focused communications, recruiting new talent, keeping sound financial records, adopting efficient technologies or creating key partnerships. When capacity building is at its best, it allows you to drive your mission forward, meet your goals and have a real impact on the community you serve.

According to Paul Connolly and Carol Lukas, authors of *Strengthening Nonprofit Performance: A Funder's Guide to Capacity Building*, organizational capacity should be addressed in six fundamental areas, all of which are critical in building and maintaining a strong, healthy nonprofit.

1. **MISSION, VISION AND STRATEGY.** These are the agents that power your purpose and direction. A strong, focused mission and a clear understanding of your organization's brand identity is key. Focused organizations keep their constituency in mind. They are able to articulate value and tie strategy to mission and organizational capacity.

Activities to help you build capacity in this area: Strategic planning, scenario planning, organizational assessment and development.

2. **GOVERNANCE AND LEADERSHIP.** A nonprofit is only as strong as those who lead it. This means you need an engaged, supportive board with the tools and resources to effectively oversee policy, mission and goals, programs, finances and the performance of the executive director. You also need a "tapped in" leader, alert to community, funder and board needs, able to recruit and retain talent and supply the resources the organization needs to thrive.

Activities to help you build capacity in this area: Leadership development, board development and executive transition planning.

▶ Capacity building can advance an organization's ability to deliver programs, expand and be adaptive and innovative. Capacity building activities include: strategic planning, technology upgrades, operational improvements and board development.

Source: *Strengthening Nonprofit Performance: A Funder's Guide to Capacity Building*, by Paul Connolly and Carol Lukas.

No. 4

3. **PROGRAM DELIVERY AND IMPACT.** Programming impact is why you're here. And effective programs are those that truly serve community needs. Evaluation should be a priority as it informs goals, highlights successes and illustrates the impact on the target constituency.

Activities to help you build capacity in this area: Program design, implementation and evaluation.

4. **STRATEGIC RELATIONSHIPS.** Relationships are everything. Strong nonprofits are led by active, committed individuals who place priority on building and maintaining alliances within the community, as well as connecting with their diverse constituencies.

Activities to help you build capacity in this area: Collaboration and strategic restructuring, marketing and communications.

5. **RESOURCE DEVELOPMENT.** To be effective, your goals and objectives should be clearly aligned with your mission. At every touchpoint, your organization should link strategic messages to resource development. Support for resource development should come from a variety of sources, creating a diverse, stable revenue flow.

Activities to help you build capacity in this area: Fund development and business planning for revenue-generating activities.

6. **INTERNAL OPERATIONS AND MANAGEMENT.** Efficient and effective operations and strong management support systems are necessary to keep your nonprofit healthy and sustainable. Sound record keeping and accounting principles should be paramount. Your organizational culture should promote open communication, transparency, respect and encourage everyone to do their best. Asset risk and technology management should also be a priority.

Activities to help you build capacity in this area: HR management and training, financial management, operations, technology systems, facility planning, legal issues, volunteer recruitment and management, conflict resolution.

At its best, capacity building allows you to drive your mission forward, meet your goals and have a real impact on the community you serve.

QUICK TIP

Q | What role does collaboration play in nonprofit management? How can resources be leveraged?

A | In the face of a changing economy, dwindling budgets and stretched-thin staff, many nonprofit leaders have recognized that they can't afford not to collaborate. As a result, organizations are seeking out opportunities to work together in new ways to leverage resources, share strengths, increase efficiencies, reduce overlap and develop scaled-up organizational models to tackle our most complex social issues. In fact, collaboration can even be appealing to funders because it increases the likelihood that they'll see a greater impact for their investment.

What does it mean to collaborate? Simply put, a collaboration is a mutually beneficial relationship with a purpose of meeting common goals. Jean Lipman-Blumen, author of *Connective Leadership: Managing in a Changing World,* calls collaborative leaders "connective" and writes "...they ethically and altruistically use the self and others as instruments for accomplishing goals."

Collaboration and partnerships come in many forms. Information sharing, shared grant writing, shared office space and administrative activities joint programming ventures, organizations that advocate together and even mergers of two or more organizations are examples. Ideally, nonprofit collaborations result in efficient uses of resources and significant cost savings for the organizations involved. The right partnerships can also bring "like-minds" together in unexpected ways to solve larger, more complex social issues.

The Fieldstone Nonprofit Guide to Forming Alliances identifies the four types of business alliances as:

- **COOPERATION:** Informal arrangements and relationships with no change in organizational structure of participating entities.

- **COORDINATION:** More formal arrangements and relationships that focus on specific programs or projects and are accompanied by plans and a shared mission.

- **COLLABORATION:** Longer-term, formal arrangements and relationships where separate organizations are brought into a new structure with a shared mission.

- **MERGER:** Arrangement in which two organizations become one.

No. 5

How to make collaborations work? Collaborations have lifecycles. In the early stages, structure is typically kept to a minimum. As the value of the collaboration increases and membership grows, more attention needs to be paid to the details. Here are some key steps to help you make your collaborations a success:

1. **KNOW YOUR ORGANIZATION, YOUR CONSTITUENCY AND YOUR GOALS.** The more able you are to articulate your mission, values, purpose and goals, the more likely you are to create collaborations that work.

2. **DEFINE THE COLLABORATION CLEARLY AND TIE IT TO GOALS AND OBJECTIVES.** Ensure each participant's purpose is understood. Define roles and responsibilities and hold individuals accountable. Build relationships based on trust and open communication.

3. **GET BUY-IN.** Involve key stakeholders and get support from those who can help move the collaboration forward and create impact.

4. **CREATE A PLAN OF ACTION AND FOLLOW IT.** Create measurable goals and evaluate outcomes as you go. Evaluation will help you determine whether to continue the collaboration and in what capacity.

For more information visit the Foundation Center's Nonprofit Collaboration Database for ways you can collaborate to fulfill your mission.
www.foundationcenter.org/gainknowledge/collaboration

❝ While relentless fundraising, well-connected boards and effective management are necessary, they are hardly sufficient. The secret to success lies in how great organizations mobilize every sector of society - government, business, nonprofits and the public - to be a force for good. ❞

- Leslie Crutchfield, Heather McLeod Grant, *Forces for Good: The Six Practices of High-Impact Nonprofits*

Collaboration allows nonprofits to leverage resources, share strengths, increase efficiencies, reduce overlap and create greater impact.

QUICK TIP

Q What does it mean to be a social entrepreneur?

A The task of clearly defining the social entrepreneur is not an easy one but those who are drawn to the service sector will recognize some familiar qualities. The Skoll Foundation defines a social entrepreneur as "society's change agent: a pioneer of innovation that benefits humanity." In *Social Entrepreneurship: The Case for Definition*, Sally Osberg and Roger Martin define a social entrepreneur as:

> *Someone who targets an equilibrium that causes the neglect, marginalization, or suffering of a segment of humanity, who brings to bear on this situation his or her inspiration, direct action, creativity, courage, and fortitude, and who aims for and ultimately affects the establishment of a new equilibrium that secures permanent benefit for the targeted group and society at large.*

And here's a summary from *The World of the Social Entrepreneur, The International Journal of Public Sector Management by J.L. Thompson:* A social entrepreneur recognizes a social problem and uses entrepreneurial strategies (typically found in the corporate world) to organize, create and manage a venture to make social change. A social entrepreneur focuses on creating social capital. Thus, the main aim of social entrepreneurship is to further social and environmental goals. Social entrepreneurs are most commonly associated with the voluntary and not-for-profit sectors, but this need not preclude making a profit.

In other words, unlike a business entrepreneur, a social entrepreneur's goal is to generate long-term social value as opposed to profit. Their focus is not only toward immediate, small-scale effects, but larger, more sustainable change.

SOCIAL ENTREPRENEURS PLAY THE ROLE OF CHANGE AGENTS IN THE SOCIAL SECTOR BY:

▸ Adopting a mission to create and sustain social value (not just private value).

▸ Recognizing and relentlessly pursuing new opportunities to serve that mission.

▸ Engaging in a process of continuous innovation, adaptation and learning.

▸ Acting boldly without being limited by resources currently in hand.

▸ Exhibiting heightened accountability to the constituencies served and for the outcomes created.

Source: *The Meaning of "Social Entrepreneurship,"* by J. Gregory Dees, 2001.

"Social entrepreneurs are not content just to give a fish or teach how to fish. They will not rest until they have revolutionized the fishing industry."
Bill Drayton, CEO, chair and founder of Ashoka

QUICK TIP

Q What are social ventures and how are they funded? What about PRIs?

A A social venture is an undertaking by a social entrepreneur seeking to provide systemic solutions to achieve a sustainable, social objective. Social ventures can be for-profit or nonprofit. What's important is that they focus on social issues and addressing ways to get society "unstuck," not just by solving the problem at hand, but rather by changing the entire system, building awareness of the solution and educating and encouraging others to get involved.

Often structured as nonprofits with wide-scale social change as a goal over profit, social entrepreneurs do face significant challenges when looking for funding for their social ventures. Potential sources can vary. If you're starting a social venture, you might consider approaching banks for loans, or corporations for funding. For example Citibank operates Citi Foundation, a grantmaking organization that may offer funding to social ventures. For-profit social ventures should think about taking advantage of angel investors and venture capital funding. And, there are a number of foundations offering seed-stage grants that can get a social venture started. Try Ashoka (www.ashoka.org) and Skoll Foundation (www.skollfoundation.org) to begin. If grants look unlikely, investigate program-related investments (PRIs), which are essentially loans by foundations.

PRI BASICS

PRIs or program-related investments are hybrid grants/loans that provide capital for charitable purposes at below market rates. Specifically,

1. A PRI helps a foundation accomplish an exempt purpose (charitable, scientific, literary, religious or educational) where the production of income or appreciation of property is not significant.

2. A PRI should not be used to influence legislation or for political purposes.

PRIs can take a number of forms such as equity investments, below-market loans or loan guarantees, and are often used by foundations to fund requests outside their grantmaking guidelines but complimentary to their core interest areas. Though grants are still the preferred choice for funding, PRIs may be a financing source for social ventures.

To learn more about PRIs, visit the IRS website.
www.irs.gov/charities/foundations/article/0,,id=137793,00.html

Q | What about innovation? How can a nonprofit go from good to great?

A | In the nonprofit world, innovation often lags behind the need to pursue everyday programming activities. But that's not to say it's not out there. Research shows many nonprofits across the country are innovating to create more impact. In fact, they often utilize similar practices to help them go from good to great.

Recently, Leslie Crutchfield and Heather McLeod Grant published a study of high-impact nonprofits and uncovered six innovative practices that any organization can use to address organizational challenges, build capacity, effectively fulfill their mission and create more impact in the communities they serve. Here's how your organization can go from good to great:

1. **ADVOCATE AND SERVE.** Innovative organizations have recognized that it's not enough simply to serve a constituency or advocate for it. Great nonprofits bridge the gap between service and advocacy and get good at doing both. This significantly increases their organizational impact.

2. **MAKE MARKETS WORK.** Innovative organizations are in bed with business. These nonprofits find ways to work with the private sector, influencing business practices, building relationships and developing earned income ventures, all in an effort to leverage the market to achieve larger scale social change.

3. **INSPIRE EVANGELISTS.** Innovative nonprofits see volunteers and donors as more than just extra hands or dollars in their pocket. These individuals are cultivated, inspired and engaged as evangelists for the cause. As committed voices, evangelists build and sustain networks of "believers" to help the nonprofit achieve larger goals.

4. **NURTURE NONPROFIT NETWORKS.** Innovative nonprofits see competitors in a different light. They're keen to build alliances, recognizing networks help people help each other. In this way, everyone thrives.

5. **MASTER THE ART OF ADAPTATION.** Innovative organizations readily listen, learn and adapt to changing conditions, modifying their strategies as needed for a better chance at success. This allows them to sustain impact by staying relevant.

6. **SHARE LEADERSHIP.** Innovative leaders share power to be a stronger force for good. Leadership is delegated appropriately throughout the organization and the network. Leaders empower staff, board and partners, motivating and driving others to participate, reach and hold themselves accountable.

Q How are boards evolving? What role does the board chair play in support of the executive director? What about succession planning?

A As our economy changes along with our social landscape, the challenges facing nonprofits are getting bigger. As a result, nonprofit boards are, by necessity, becoming more diverse, strategic and engaged.

In the past, board responsibilities were viewed as volunteer work and not held to the same standards as for-profit boards. For this reason, members often held more passive roles, tasked with setting policy, receiving reports and approving management's plans and strategies. To be effective today, board members must take their roles and responsibilities very seriously, as they work hand in hand with the executive director to guide policy, connect with the community, provide financial oversight and strategic support, implement programs and meet goals and objectives.

> Board members must work strategically with the executive director to guide policy, connect with community, provide financial oversight and strategic support, implement programs and meet goals.

More than ever before, today's board does work that matters. The authors of a *Harvard Business Review* article called "The New Work of the Nonprofit Board" explain that boards have evolved over the years to concern themselves with crucial "do or die" issues central to the institution's success, impact and reach.

Today's boards work with management to set and implement policy and agendas and solve problems together. They are goal driven, defining clear measures of success; the actions of members are driven by strategic priorities and circumstance; and they require the engagement of the organizations' internal and external constituencies. Today's board chair is committed to operating under the guiding principle of what's best for the organization. He or she facilitates board leadership and good governance. In this way, the chair molds the board's culture, direction and impact.

For this reason, the relationship between the board chair and the executive director is critical, as the two — collaboratively — drive the organization's mission forward. Here, trust is key. Communication should be open and candid, and each should rely on the other's strengths in pursuit of their common goal. Both the executive director and the chair should also have clearly defined roles and responsibilities so that everyone understands where one individual's authority ends and the other person's begins. This helps to determine what issues matter for the board, and what issues lie in the domain of the organization itself. Adapted in part from *BoardSource* and the *Board Chair Handbook, Second Edition* (www.boardsource.org).

Succession planning is another leadership area in which the board should be very involved. Often, organizations focus on covering immediate needs, expecting to put a succession plan in place if the executive director announces his or her departure. But what happens if that departure is unexpected? Have others been groomed for leadership roles? Does the executive director hold critical relationships that couldn't be quickly taken over by someone else? Will the board know what actions to take when the time comes? It's also worth noting that change is inevitable. There may be other management, staff or board positions that should be considered in a succession plan.

In the Free Management Library (www.managementhelp.org), HR expert Sheri Mazurek offers the following tips for succession planning:

- Do not wait until the employee will be leaving.

- Focus on policies, procedures and practices, not on personalities.

- Succession planning is a responsibility of the management, not just the employee.

- Succession planning should be in accordance with up-to-date personnel policies.

To learn more about board leadership read Chapter 3: Boards and Governance.

❝ Individually we are one drop,
together we are an ocean. ❞

- Ryunosuke Satoro, Poet

NO. **10**

Q } Is nonprofit sustainability a reality?

A } The nonprofit landscape is changing and you're faced with a real challenge. You want to create impact and build a sustainable future for your nonprofit. But is it really possible? Experts say, yes! In fact, Jeanne Bell, Jan Masaoka and Steve Zimmerman, authors of *Nonprofit Sustainability: Making Strategic Decisions for Financial Viability,* say that when nonprofits begin to understand how to bring programmatic goals together with financial goals, they'll start to make decisions that lead to organizational sustainability. These experts say that sustainable nonprofits follow these core principles:

▸ Keep in mind, succession planning is also a critical aspect of sustainability! It ensures that staff, leadership and board members don't take critical knowledge and relationships with them when they leave.

1. **FINANCIAL SUSTAINABILITY.** Sustainable nonprofits always tie impact goals to financial goals. Remember, fiscal health and the maintenance of adequate working capital is as intrinsic to success over the long term as community impact is.

2. **EFFECTIVE MANAGEMENT OF HYBRID REVENUE STRATEGIES.** Nonprofits today are supported by diverse sources. Many nonprofits are looking at alternative revenue-producing models to mitigate funding cuts. Management of hybrid strategies can be a challenge. For this reason, different financial goals must be set for different revenue streams and each must be managed in a different way.

3. **DEVELOPMENT OF AN EXPLICIT NONPROFIT BUSINESS MODEL.** Strategic business decisions can't be made without an existing business model. For this reason, every nonprofit needs to develop a viable business strategy that brings together all of the organization's activities under the umbrella of the organization's mission. In the nonprofit world, programmatic impact strategies will be a significant part of the business model. But each activity should be associated not only with an impact strategy but also a revenue strategy. Thus, the sustainable nonprofit has a "dual bottom-line" — impact and financial return.

4. **CONTINUOUS DECISION-MAKING.** Today's nonprofits face unprecedented challenges. Evaluation, assessment and continuous decision-making are necessary for survival and success when change is constant.

According to Jeanne Bell et al., "Sustainability is not a destination or a solution. It is a direction and an orientation requiring continuous decision-making that reflects the dynamic context in which nonprofits operate."

LEADERSHIP

- **Alliance for Nonprofit Management**
  (www.allianceonline.org)

- **Annie E. Casey Foundation**
  (www.aecf.org)

- **Aspen Institute**
  (www.aspeninstitute.org)

- **The Bridgespan Group**
  (www.bridgespan.org)

- **Center for Creative Leadership**
  (www.ccl.org)

- **Center for Nonprofit Advancement**
  (www.nonprofitadvancement.org)

- **CompassPoint Nonprofit Services**
  (www.compasspoint.org)

- **Free Management Library**
  (www.managementhelp.org)

- **Leader to Leader Institute**
  (www.pfdf.org)

- **Nonprofit Management Education Resources**
  (www.uwex.edu/ces/cced/nonprofits/
  management/index.cfm)

- **Rockwood Leadership Institute**
  (www.rockwoodleadership.org)

- **Social Justice Leadership**
  (www.sojustlead.org)

- **Working Across Generations**
  (www.workingacrossgenerations.org)

BLOGS

- **Learning Leadership**
  (www.christopherscottblog.typepad.com/blog)

- **Mission-Based Management**
  (www.missionbased.blogspot.com)

- **Nonprofit Leadership**
  (www.nonprofitalternatives.org/page)

- **Nonprofit News and Comment: The Hauser
  Center for Nonprofit Organizations at
  Harvard University**
  (www.hausercenter.org/npnews)

BOOKS

- *Execution: The Discipline of Getting Things
  Done,* by Larry Bossidy, Ram Charan and
  Charles Burck

- *"Inside the Foundation: Program-Related
  Investments," To Improve Health and Health
  Care, Volume V (The Robert Wood Johnson
  Foundation Anthology),* by Stephen L. Isaacs
  and James R. Knickman, eds.

- *The Jossey-Bass Handbook of Nonprofit
  Leadership and Management,* by Robert D.
  Herman & Associates

- *Leadership and the One Minute Manager,*
  by Ken Blanchard, Patricia Zigarmi and
  Drea Zigarmi

- *Learning to Lead: A Workbook on Becoming a
  Leader,* by Warren Bennis and Joan Goldsmith

- *Program-Related Investing: Skills and
  Strategies for New PRI Funders (GrantCraft
  Series),* by Neil Carlson

- *Reframing Organizations: Artistry, Choice
  and Leadership (Jossey-Bass Business &
  Management Series),* by Lee G. Bolman and
  Terrence E. Deal

READY-TO-GO-RESOURCES

20-SECOND-SUMMARY

- Leadership is an art. It goes without saying that an effective leader needs to have vision and passion along with the analytical and technical skills necessary to do the job. It's more than just managing. Emotional competence is really the key to putting it all into practice.

- Strengthen your nonprofit, drive your mission forward and meet your goals! Seek out capacity building services in your community. Look for coaching and consulting services, organizational assessment services, training and workshops and peer networks.

- Organizations all across the country are using innovative practices to create more impact. Inspire evangelists for your cause, master the art of adaptation and nurture your nonprofit networks – and you too can take your nonprofit from good to great.

- Use collaboration and partnership as opportunities to leverage resources, share strengths and give your organization a fighting chance at sustainability.

- Nonprofit sustainability is achievable as long as you reconcile programmatic goals with financial goals.

2

LEGAL

The decision to start and run a nonprofit may be one of the most important choices you'll ever make.

It usually takes a substantial commitment of time and energy, and requires that the interests of the mission be placed ahead of your individual interests. Establishing your legal structure and applying for tax-exempt status can be a major headache. However, taking the proper steps will help to position your organization for success in the long run.

Gaining 501(c)(3) status is only the beginning of your journey. Once you've launched, you'll need to understand a complex web of federal and state laws. Some — like employment laws — apply to any organization. Others apply uniquely to nonprofits and are conditions to maintain your tax-exempt status. Carefully addressing legal requirements will provide a solid foundation for carrying out your work. To support you in that effort, this chapter addresses common questions related to legally forming and operating a nonprofit organization.

DISCLAIMER: The information contained in this book is general in nature and may not be applicable to all situations. In addition, federal and state laws change. You should refer to the most current editions of additional resources listed for each topic and consult with an attorney or accountant on important matters.

Q | How do we form a nonprofit organization?

A You've got the passion, the knowledge and the resources to get started. But how do you actually set up a nonprofit organization?

First, it's important to understand what a nonprofit is from a legal standpoint. A nonprofit is simply an organization that does not distribute profits to shareholders. However, when most people refer to nonprofits, they are talking about recognized tax-exempt organizations.

Here, we'll discuss the formation of an organization structured as a California Nonprofit Public Benefit Corporation, organized for charitable purposes and exempt under Internal Revenue Code §501(c)(3) and §23701d of the California Revenue and Taxation Code.

BEFORE YOU BEGIN.

It's important to note that there are many steps you'll need to take prior to legally forming a nonprofit corporation. While you are likely eager to get your mission-driven charitable endeavor off the ground, failure to adequately research the need for your programs and services, and determine fundraising feasibility, will ultimately undermine your efforts.

It's also possible that your planning phase will reveal alternative legal structures that are better suited to your needs. See question 2 in this section for a discussion of other legal structures.

SETTING UP YOUR LEGAL STRUCTURE.

The legal process of forming a nonprofit starts with filing for both federal and state tax-exempt status. At the federal level, this is done through the Internal Revenue Service. Filing with the state in which your nonprofit is located is done through that state's department of revenue. Keep in mind, while this discussion of federal designation applies to organizations anywhere in the United States, each individual state also has its own laws, so be sure to refer to your specific state laws before you begin.

▶ Forming a nonprofit corporation is one of the last steps to take in preparing to launch your organization. Careful research and advance planning will benefit your mission far more than a tax determination letter will.

Each state has it's own laws surrounding setting up a nonprofit, so be sure to check your state laws before you file for tax exempt status.

QUICK TIP

No. 1

The following steps will help you incorporate a nonprofit organization and obtain tax exemption from the Franchise Tax Board and Internal Revenue Service (IRS):

- Prepare articles of incorporation and file them with the Secretary of State. This process typically takes 10-12 weeks if filed by mail and 2-3 weeks if hand-delivered to Los Angeles or Sacramento.

- Prepare your organization's bylaws.

- Apply for an Employer Identification Number (EIN) with the IRS. This process typically takes 30 days.

- In California: Register with the California Attorney General's Registry of Charitable Trusts. California charities must register within 30 days after receiving their first assets.

- Recruit a board of directors and conduct an initial meeting. At this time, directors will accept their role, adopt or ratify bylaws, elect officers and authorize application for tax exemption. You'll also want to create bank accounts and complete other steps necessary to begin operations.

- Apply to the IRS for recognition of federal tax exemption. This process typically takes 90 days.

The legal process of incorporating and obtaining tax-exempt status is arduous and time-consuming. The steps outlined above note the average processing time for each application, assuming that application materials are complete and that requests for additional information are readily addressed. Regardless of how thorough you are, know that obtaining nonprofit status will take time.

To help navigate the process, you may want to hire an attorney familiar with nonprofit law to assist in preparing and submitting required materials. This can be particularly beneficial if you want to speed up your application or if you encounter problems preparing the required documentation.

Visit www.nonprofitanswerguide.org for timely sector resources and more expert answers to your most immediate nonprofit questions.

QUICK TIP

Q | What other legal structures are there for nonprofits? What about fiscal sponsors?

A | During your planning phase, you may determine that an alternative legal structure is better suited to your organization's needs. In addition to forming a nonprofit corporation as described in question 1, there are four common alternatives.

1. You can form an unincorporated association.

2. You can form a limited liability company.

3. You can be incubated by a fiscal sponsor.

4. You can become affiliated with another nonprofit.

While the law does not require organizations to be incorporated in order to be eligible for tax exemption, unincorporated associations cannot offer protection against personal liability to directors and members. In addition, while there may be fewer reporting requirements of unincorporated associations, many foundations are not willing to fund them.

Technically speaking, a nonprofit can be formed as a limited liability company, or LLC. As of 2004, this is legal in California and qualified organizations can gain tax-exempt status. However, the requirements to gain federal 501(c)(3) status as an LLC frequently disqualify many interested organizations. IRS regulations prohibit individuals as members of the LLC and only allow members that are themselves exempt organizations. In other words, your organization would already have to be a legally recognized 501(c)(3) in order to apply for federal tax-exempt status as an LLC.

Fiscal sponsorship is an approach that allows an organization with 501(c)(3) status to extend its legal status to another organization (or initiative or project). Many such organizations offer administrative support and technical assistance to help advance an organization's goals, generally at low cost. This option provides an opportunity to

▷ Don't just assume a 501(c)(3) structure is the answer. There are several other options that may make more sense for your organization, at least in the beginning. Take the time to research your options and determine what's best for your specific situation.

Check with your state's Office of the Secretary of State to find out specific legal structures allowed where your nonprofit will operate.

QUICK TIP

grow your start-up project and legally accept grants and donations without the red tape associated with establishing a stand-alone entity. Once your program is established, it can transition from the incubator to become a freestanding organization.

Affiliation with an existing nonprofit is another option that may be available to you. If your mission and goals align closely or compliment with those of another organization, affiliation may be a wise choice. Potential benefits include a ready source of clients, access to knowledgeable staff and a "home" for your program. When looking at this option, you should consider how well the affiliate's goals match those of your program, as well as the level of autonomy your program or organization will have within that structure. Also look at the strength of existing relationships with the board, director and staff and the impact of any financial arrangements you'll make.

There are many other types of federally exempt organizations allowable by the IRS. For a complete list, refer to IRS Publication 557, Tax-Exempt Status for Your Organization.

You should also know that there are many other types of for-profit and profit/nonprofit hybrid structures that vary from state to state. For example, several states allow for the creation of low-profit limited liability companies, or L3Cs, to meet the needs of social ventures. Another option is a B Corporation, which is structured to create benefit for both society and shareholders.

When choosing a legal structure for your organization, it's highly recommended that you consult with an attorney experienced in tax and corporate law governing nonprofit organizations.

❝ I don't think you ever stop giving. I really don't. I think it's an on-going process. And it's not just about being able to write a check. It's being able to touch somebody's life.❞

- Oprah Winfrey

Find a complete list of federally exempt organizations allowable by the IRS in IRS Publication 557, Tax-Exempt Status for your organization.

QUICK TIP

Q | What forms must be filed by a nonprofit each year?

A | You're busy starting and running your nonprofit and the last thing you want to think about is filing. But the IRS and the Franchise Tax Board take filing deadlines and requirements very seriously, so you should too.

All tax-exempt organizations must file a federal return or returns. In California, all tax-exempt organizations must also file a state return or returns. Failure to do so for three consecutive years will cause your tax-exempt status to be automatically revoked by the Franchise Tax Board and the IRS.

For tax years ending on or after December 31, 2010, exempt organizations that normally have more than $50,000 in gross receipts must file either:

- Form 990, Return of Organization Exempt from Income Tax, or

- Form 990-EZ, Short Form Return of Organization Exempt from Income Tax

Exempt organizations that normally have less than $50,000 in gross receipts are eligible to file a Form 990-N (e-postcard) or they may elect to file a full return (Form 990 or 990-EZ).

"Normal" receipts are established based on an average over three years. Prior to December 31, 2010, the threshold for filing the 990-N (e-postcard) was normal gross receipts of less than $25,000. This means that there is a phase-in period to reach the current $50,000 threshold. For assistance on which forms to file, visit www.irs.gov/charities/article/0,,id=184445,00.html.

In the state of California, common forms required of tax-exempt organizations include:

- Form 199, California Exempt Organization Annual Information Return (for organizations with gross receipts normally greater than $25,000).

- Form 199N, Annual Electronic Filing Requirement for Small Exempt Organizations (for organizations with gross receipts normally equal to or less than $25,000).

- Form 109, California Exempt Organization Business Income Tax Return (for organizations with unrelated business taxable income greater than $1,000).

- Form 100, California Corporation Franchise or Income Tax Return (for organizations with taxable income greater than $100).

DON'T FORGET TO FILE!

▶ Every federally designated tax-exempt organization must file an annual return with the IRS. Failure to do so over three consecutive years will result in automatic revocation of tax-exempt status.

NO.
4

Q | Can nonprofits charge a fee for services?

A | The short answer is, yes! In fact, revenue-generating activities can be a critical component of your effort to build a sustainable nonprofit organization. Many nonprofits have found ways to create a revenue stream that flows from their programmatic work. Examples include fees for membership, direct services, publications and nonprofit-organized conferences and seminars.

The law sets no limits on the fees you can charge, although there are several factors to consider when establishing the fee for a particular service. First and foremost, the service being offered must be related to your mission. Otherwise, the revenues should be reported as unrelated business income (see question 9 in this chapter for a further discussion of related vs. unrelated income).

You should also consider the environment in which a fee is being charged. Factors such as the availability of philanthropic or sponsorship support, the full cost of the product or service, market prices for similar services and your constituents' ability to pay should be taken into account when establishing a reasonable fee.

TO SET FEES FOR SERVICE, FOLLOW THESE EASY STEPS:

1. Prioritize your objectives in charging a fee. Why do you need to charge for this particular product or service?

2. Determine the service unit cost.

3. Survey the market price of similar goods and services. What are your competitors charging?

4. Determine a percentage of costs to be recovered by fees. How much do you need to make to cover your costs?

5. Define the fee structure and discounts. For example, will you offer discounts based on a sliding scale?

6. Assess the target market's reaction to the fee. Test your pricing with your constituents.

7. Adopt a fee policy. Use this policy moving forward with additional products and services.

8. Develop implementation/collection procedures.

9. Evaluate and revise, as appropriate.

Adapted from: *Charging a Just Fee: A Guidebook for Nonprofit Organizations,* by Walter Moreau.

▶ A nonprofit can absolutely charge a fee for services. The most important things to consider are whether the service is related to your mission and the reasonable amount to charge for the service.

Q How do we reduce our risks? What kinds of insurance do we need?

A Doing good work in the community is not enough protection against possible risks. Like other small businesses, nonprofits need to have proper insurance coverage. An independent insurance agent with experience in policies for nonprofits can help. Remember, these agents only get paid based on commission on policies sold, so there is no cost associated with shopping around. Ask colleagues in the nonprofit world for recommendations or inquire with your attorney.

A qualified agent or attorney will also be in a position to help you establish a sound risk management program, including identification of loss exposure, measures to reduce loss and insurance best suited to your situation.

In many states, insurance tailored to nonprofits is offered through trade organizations or alliances that are themselves 501(c)(3)s. Such an organization could provide a useful local resource to research and identify your needs and options.

That said, there are several standard policies you'll likely need. These include General Liability, Auto Liability, Social Service Professional Liability and Directors & Officers Liability. Depending on your situation, you may also want to consider coverage for volunteers.

Other types of coverage that may be important to your specific organization include:

- Professional malpractice.

- Non-owned or hired auto liability (such as for use of employee or volunteer-owned autos).

- Improper sexual conduct for both the organization and alleged employee or volunteer perpetrator.

- Student/volunteer/participant accident.

Looking for insurance? Seek out trade organizations or 501 (c)(3) alliances offering insurance tailored to nonprofits.

QUICK TIP

No.
6

Q } Do we need a conflict of interest
policy for our board of directors?

A You want to safeguard against conflict of interest
situations in your organization, but do you really need a
policy to do so? Federal law does not require tax-exempt organizations
to have a conflict of interest policy in place. However, the IRS
strongly encourages it. Such a policy can reduce the appearance
of impropriety and help to ensure that the exempt organization
is conducting business in a manner that is consistent with its
charitable purpose.

It's important to note that conflicts of interest involving a director are
not in and of themselves illegal or improper. They are, in fact, quite
common. It's the manner in which the director and board deal with
and disclose the conflict that determines the propriety of a decision
or transaction.

So what exactly is a conflict of interest? A conflict is present whenever
a transaction has the potential to personally benefit a director.
This can occur, for example, when a director has an employment,
investment or family involvement with an entity with which the
nonprofit is dealing.

A board member's duty is to act in good faith with regard to the best
interests of the exempt organization, not in the board member's
personal interest. This is called "duty of loyalty" in the law, and
directors are legally bound to carry it out.

Given the risks and responsibilities, a written conflict of interest
policy is strongly recommended. A policy clearly spells out the legal
procedures for disclosure of conflict of interest and approving
transactions in which a director may have an interest. The board
may also wish to go beyond what the law requires and establish
more stringent policies, such as forbidding transactions in which the
director has an interest.

Adapted in part from: *Guidebook for Directors of Nonprofit Organizations*, by the American
Bar Association.

**A conflict of interest is not inherently improper. In fact, it's common.
What matters is how the conflict is disclosed and addressed.**

QUICK TIP

Q | What documents are needed for board meetings? What should be retained and for how long? What should be recorded in board minutes?

A As an exempt organization, you've been keeping an official board book. It should include all corporate documentation such as bylaws, articles of incorporation, conflict of interest policy, a template for board meeting minutes, minutes of board and committee meetings, contact information for all directors and any other documents that govern your operations.

HOW LONG YOU SHOULD KEEP YOUR RECORDS.

The IRS says that you "must keep all of your records as long as they may be needed." While this may sound like rather loose guidance, it is easy enough to determine how long that might be. Financial records, such as general ledgers and audits, should be kept for seven years. This standard is derived from the ability of the IRS to audit your records for intentional fraud for up to six years; the seventh year is needed to cover starting balances.

Corporate records, which set forth policy decisions such as board minutes, should be kept forever. The goal here is to present a full history of the organization, since an organization may need to review historic decisions (for example, the restrictions placed on a donation).

Minutes of board and committee meetings must be kept within an official board book and a tax-exempt organization is required by law to keep them. All board members should receive copies of the minutes and have access to the minutes at any time.

WHAT YOU SHOULD KNOW ABOUT MINUTES.

Minutes are the permanent record of the proceedings of a board or committee meeting. They need to be clear, accurate, brief and objective. And, they should be made available to all board members at any time.

WHAT TO INCLUDE IN MEETING MINUTES:

▸ Basic information - date, time and location, names of members present or absent, vote results

▸ Name of persons abstaining from any vote or requesting that their vote be recorded

▸ Names of members who disclosed a potential conflict of interest, the nature of the conflict and disposition

▸ A list of all reports and documents introduced during the meeting (with copies attached)

▸ A summary of significant points raised

Adapted from: *10 Minutes to Better Board Meetings,* by Planned Parenthood Federation of America.

Q | Can a nonprofit lobby?

A First and foremost, it's important to understand how the law defines lobbying. The IRS refers to lobbying as "influencing legislation." This is done *directly* (as in communicating directly with a legislator or their staff to express a view about specific legislation) or *indirectly* (such as communicating with members, encouraging target audiences to contact legislators or speaking with the media about specific legislation).

A great deal of advocacy does not fall within the definition of lobbying. For example, a 501(c)(3) is permitted to make the results of nonpartisan research available or broadly discuss social issues. A complete list of permitted activities is available in IRS Publication 557.

Generally speaking, a 501(c)(3) public-benefit charity is not allowed to make lobbying a "substantial part" of its activities. Unfortunately, this statement is ambiguous at best. In the past, courts have found expenditures of more than 5 percent of an organization's budget, time and effort to be "substantial."

A far more defined test is outlined in §501(h) of the Internal Revenue Code. This sets specific dollar limits on an organization's lobbying activities and counts only lobbying expenditures (money and staff time) toward those limits. In most cases, this will enable an organization to engage in more lobbying activity with greater security that it will not endanger its tax-exempt status. To do so, you must file IRS form 5768 within the first tax year to which the form applies.

It's also important to note that all 501(c)(3) organizations are prohibited from campaigning for or against a candidate for elected office.

Private foundations are absolutely prohibited from lobbying. Grant agreements will typically include language noting that the recipient organization agrees to not use any of the granted funds for lobbying activity.

> If you do any kind of advocacy at all, to ensure you keep your tax-exempt status, get up to speed on what the law says lobbying is and isn't. The good news is, a lot of options are available to you and most of what you do to educate will not be considered lobbying.

Check with the IRS before lobbying. While it is allowed in certain instances, a nonprofit is never allowed to intervene in a political campaign.

QUICK TIP

Q | What is the difference between a "related" and "unrelated" business activity?

A You want to bring in more revenue and you're thinking about your options. Before you begin, you'll need to understand how your business activities are perceived from a tax perspective.

When a nonprofit charges a fee for a service or sells a product as an ongoing activity, the law considers whether the activity or product is "related" to the organization's mission. If the business is "related" to your exempt purposes, then you will not incur corporate income taxes on the net proceeds of that business activity (though you may need to pay sales and other taxes).

Taking care to ensure that your business is "related" reduces the risk that your organization will lose its tax exemption for carrying on too much activity that does not further the mission.

An example of "related" business would be a health clinic that charges patients a reduced price for health services. This furthers its mission to provide affordable health care services.

If the business is not related to your exempt purposes, then it is considered "unrelated" and net income is subject to Unrelated Business Income Tax (UBIT). UBIT is applied when gross income from the unrelated business is $1,000 or more. These are reported and paid by filing a Form 990-T, which is required in addition to any other tax forms required of the exempt organization. Individual states may also have their own filing and tax requirements. For example, in California, the Franchise Tax Board requires a Form 109 to pay tax on unrelated business.

Keep in mind, there are limitations on the amount of unrelated business activity in which a nonprofit can engage. Under IRS regulations, a nonprofit risks losing its tax exemption if an unrelated business constitutes a "substantial" portion of the organization's total activities. While the word "substantial" is subject to interpretation, if the unrelated business activity grows to 25 percent of your nonprofit organization's activity, you should seek legal counsel. One option for continuing to engage in a substantial amount of unrelated business activity is to form a subsidiary corporation or limited liability company to carry on the business.

This is a brief description of a complex area. If your organization is carrying on or planning to start a business venture, the advice of legal counsel familiar with these complicated tax rules is strongly advised.

STILL NOT SURE IF YOUR ACTIVITY IS RELATED?

Know that the IRS considers an activity to be "unrelated" if all three of the following are present:

▸ It is a trade or business (i.e., selling of goods or services).

▸ It is regularly carried on (as distinct from the occasional car wash or bake sale).

▸ It is not substantially related to furthering the exempt purpose of the organization.

No. **10**

Q Does the IRS regulate how much a nonprofit can pay its employees?

A When you're a nonprofit administrator or director setting salaries for your employees, you're accountable to many parties, and the IRS is one of them. While the IRS doesn't regulate specific compensation amounts, it does require that tax-exempt organizations limit the salaries and benefits of executives and staff to "reasonable compensation." In fact, you'll need to list compensation of officers, directors, trustees, key employees and others on your 990 federal tax return.

But what is "reasonable"? Simply put, "reasonable" means that the amount of compensation is approximate to what would be provided by a similar organization in similar circumstances. In other words, the IRS expects you to do some homework to understand the going rate for a comparable position.

As a general guideline, all nonprofits should be prepared to justify how the amount of salary was determined for any senior staff or "significant" position. An annual salary of $50,000 in addition to fringe benefits is a useful benchmark to identify significant positions. In addition, if audited, your nonprofit organization will need to show comparables. The Center for Nonprofit Management produces an annual Compensation & Benefits Survey that can be especially useful in determining appropriate compensation.

To learn more, visit www.cnmsocal.org.

Not sure what level of compensation is appropriate? CNM's annual Compensation and Benefits Survey can help! Purchase it at www.cnmsocal.org.

QUICK TIP

- **Governance and Related Topics - 501(c)(3) Organizations:**
www.irs.gov/pub/irs-tege/governance_practices.pdf

- **Governance Check Sheet:**
www.irs.gov/pub/irs-tege/governance_check_sheet.pdf

- **IRS FAQs about the Annual Reporting Requirements for Exempt Organizations:**
www.irs.gov/charities/article/0,,id=96581,00.html

- **IRS Form 990 Series - Which Form to File:**
www.irs.gov/charities/article/0,,id=184445,00.html

- **IRS Form 1023, Application for Recognition of Exemption Under Section 501(c)(3) of the Internal Revenue Code:**
www.irs.gov/pub/irs-pdf/f1023.pdf

- **IRS Publication 557, Tax-Exempt Status for Your Organization:**
www.irs.gov/pub/irs-pdf/p557.pdf

- **IRS Publication 598, Tax on Unrelated Business Income of Exempt Organizations:**
www.irs.gov/pub/irs-pdf/p598.pdf

- **Tips and samples for filing articles of incorporation with the California Secretary of State:**
www.sos.ca.gov/business/corp/pdf/articles/corp_artsnp.pdf

- **California Attorney General's Guide for Charities:**
www.ag.ca.gov/charities/publications/guide_for_charities.pdf

- **Form 3500, California Exemption Application Booklet:**
www.ftb.ca.gov/forms/misc/3500bk.pdf

- **Franchise Tax Board Publication 1068, Exempt Organizations – Filing Requirements and Filing Fees:**
www.ftb.ca.gov/forms/misc/1068.pdf

- **Center for Nonprofit Management Compensation & Benefits Survey:**
www.cnmsocal.org/salarysurvey.html

- *How to Form a Nonprofit Corporation in California,* by Anthony Mancuso

20-SECOND-SUMMARY

- Laws do apply to nonprofit organizations. In fact, they are often held to higher standards and more rigid reporting requirements because of their tax-exempt status. Become familiar with relevant laws and keep apprised of changes.

- When launching a nonprofit endeavor, take your time and do your homework. Resist the urge to rush. The red tape and time associated with legal formation can be frustrating, but it's most important to establish a viable program focus and identify the appropriate legal structure.

- Plan to keep your corporate records – those that set forth policy decisions – forever.

- Be prepared to justify the salary and benefits of staff. Failure to do so can be extremely costly.

- When in doubt, consult an attorney experienced with nonprofits. Remember that the law changes regularly so keeping up-to-date will be essential.

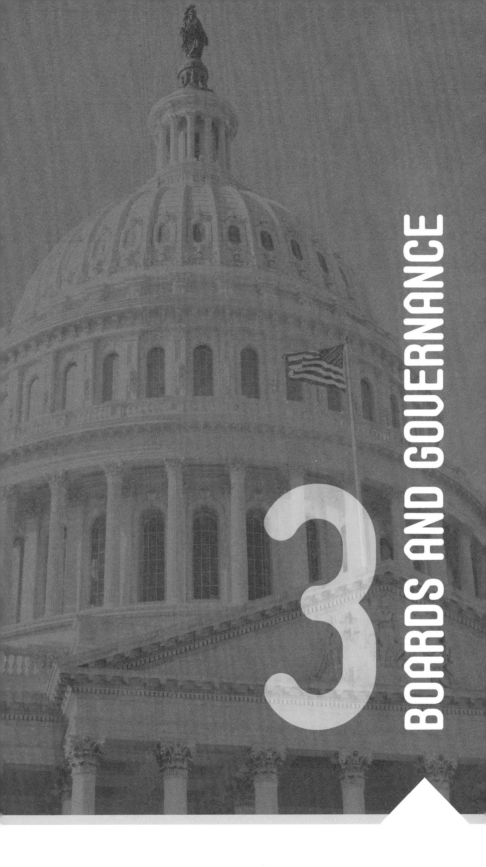

3
BOARDS AND GOVERNANCE

30-SECOND-OVERVIEW

Serving on a nonprofit board can be an incredibly rewarding experience.

But it isn't a responsibility to be taken lightly. In the past decade, government has implemented rigorous rules that govern the actions of boards of public companies. These have inspired many state laws that apply to your nonprofit. And, public expectation for good governance is greater than ever before.

This chapter addresses the legal and ethical responsibilities that come with being a board member. We also look at best practices related to board operations, recruitment, financial oversight, fundraising and internal communications. This is the business side of any nonprofit, and it all leads to greater effectiveness of one of your most powerful assets: your nonprofit board.

Q } What are the basic responsibilities of a board and the legal duties of board members?

A } The board is legally responsible for the operation of the nonprofit organization for which it serves. In fact, individual members can even be held personally liable for improper conduct if they breach their duties. So, pay careful attention to the law and board duties. Doing so will help you minimize risk and ensure your organization is the best it can be.

STANDARDS OF CONDUCT

Under the law, each board member must meet certain standards of conduct. These standards are typically described as duty of care, duty of loyalty and duty of obedience.

1. **DUTY OF CARE.** A board member must exercise "reasonable care" when he or she makes a decision for the organization. In this case, "reasonable" is what a prudent person in a similar situation might do.

2. **DUTY OF LOYALTY.** A board member must never use information gained through his or her position for personal gain. This means each member must always act in the best interests of the organization.

3. **DUTY OF OBEDIENCE.** A board member must be faithful to the organization's mission. This means he or she cannot act in a way that is inconsistent with the organization's goals.

BOARD RESPONSIBILITIES

In addition to standards of conduct, as a governing body, the board has a responsibility to support management and staff, and ensure operations run smoothly and in accordance with the law. Following are 10 responsibilities of nonprofit boards.

1. Establish mission and purpose.

2. Select the executive director.

3. Support and evaluate the executive director.

4. Set policies and ensure effective planning.

5. Monitor and strengthen programs and services.

6. Ensure adequate financial resources.

▶ Serving on a board is a serious responsibility. Each board member must follow conflict of interest and confidentiality rules and assist the board in carrying out its fiduciary responsibilities. This includes reviewing financial statements and monitoring income and expenditures.

7. Protect assets and provide proper financial oversight.

8. Build a competent board.

9. Ensure legal and ethical integrity.

10. Enhance the organization's public standing.

Source: *Ten Basic Responsibilities of Nonprofit Boards, Second Edition,* by Richard T. Ingram (BoardSource 2009)

LAWS AND GUIDELINES GOVERNING BOARDS

In 2002, the U.S. government passed the American Competitiveness and Corporate Accountability Act (a.k.a. the Sarbanes-Oxley Act), which regulates the financial controls of corporate boards.

The Act itself doesn't apply to nonprofits, but there are a number of provisions you might want to adopt voluntarily, particularly as they relate to board oversight and committees, disclosure, document retention, whistleblower policies and audits. We're not alone in this recommendation. In its publication, Compliance Guide for 501(c)(3) Public Charities, the Internal Revenue Service recommends that nonprofits consider whether such governance practices are necessary to ensure sound operations and compliance with tax law.

It's also important to note that Sarbanes-Oxley may be relevant to your nonprofit in that it inspired a number of state laws that govern nonprofits, such as the California Nonprofit Integrity Act of 2004, which addresses registration of a charity, financial reporting, auditing and other areas relevant to a nonprofit's finances and management. And remember, state laws vary, so it's important that you become familiar with relevant legislation in your area of operations.

▶ The board of directors establishes fundamental policies that guide decision making in the organization. Such policies include mission and values, goals and priorities, primary constituency and types of service. Decisions that govern ongoing operations — such as day-to-day planning, operating procedures, and rules that guide conduct — are typically developed at the organizational level.

Individual members can be held liable for improper conduct if they breach their duties. To minimize risk, pay careful attention to the law and board duties.

QUICK TIP

Q How does the board ensure the organization is mission driven?

A A mission-driven organization is one that is constituent-focused at every touchpoint. Your mission may be defined in terms of providing exemplary service, or developing products that meet and exceed the needs of your target audiences, or both.

A mission-driven strategy can be a framework to help your board align your programs and services with the values and priorities of your organization. But how do you ensure your board is using this framework effectively?

First, the executive director and the board should establish a guiding mission and vision that reflect the organization's unique purpose. This will require careful research and strategic planning. It's important that the executive director and staff support the board with the research they need in order to develop a clear mission that positions your organization appropriately and sets you up for success.

Once established, board commitment to driving your mission forward at every opportunity is essential. Such a commitment helps everyone in the organization create a solid operational structure, a strong organizational identity and effective communications and fundraising strategies.

Here are three tips to ensure your board keeps your organization's mission top priority.

1. DEVELOP OPPORTUNITIES TO KEEP BOARD MEMBERS COMMUNICATING. Members should be engaged in moving your mission forward. Keep the line of communication open between board members and the executive director to encourage a spirit of inquiry and a shared understanding of your common purpose.

2. ASK THE BOARD TO REGULARLY REVIEW COMMUNICATIONS AND FUNDRAISING PLANS. Ensure they tie in with mission and strategic goals. This keeps them tied into critical organizational priorities and ensures the mission is top of mind for everyone. Be sure to follow up on their suggestions for refinement or improvement.

3. DON'T LET YOUR "MISSION DRIFT." Potential support from large donors or corporate sponsors can sometimes result in taking on programming that is not in line with your mission. If growth means a potential shift, do your research and plan your strategies before you make the leap.

TO GUARD AGAINST
AN UNCLEAR OR
MISGUIDED MISSION,
ASK YOURSELF:

▶ What is the unique social benefit provided by our organization and how important is it to the community?

▶ Does our mission have meaning for stakeholders, or is it just boilerplate for grant applications?

▶ Do we know our organization's competitive advantage, and who our constituents are?

Source: *Mission-Driven Governance*, by Raymond Fisman, Rakesh Khurana and Edward Martenson

No.
3

Q ⟩ What are some best practices for board operations?

A ⟩ Implementing "best practices" for building and running a board effectively can help you further your cause with confidence. Here are some top issues to consider.

BOARD SIZE

Federal law doesn't dictate board size, but state laws often establish a minimum (typically one to three members).

Beyond legal requirements, the number of board members will depend largely on your organization's needs. Before you decide on size, it's best to think about your needs. Do you want to create a diverse board with varied skills, knowledge and experience to support your organization and match the needs of a diverse constituency? To determine the right number for your organization, think about the dynamics between members and their ability to accomplish tasks. Consider whether adding more will help or hinder in this regard.

QUORUM

A quorum is the minimum number of members that must be present at a meeting to make the proceedings of that meeting valid. This is typically established in an organization's bylaws, although in some cases state law will determine the quorum. Often the quorum for a meeting of the board is one-third of its total members, or two directors (whichever is higher).

EFFECTIVE MEETING PLANNING

To ensure full participation and thoughtful decision making in the best interest of the organization, board meetings should always be carefully planned, facilitated and documented for implementation and follow-up.

Here's how you can keep meetings on track:

BEGIN WITH A CLEAR, FOCUSED AGENDA. Agendas should address meeting topics and outline goals for discussion. Deliver the agenda to board members at least a week in advance. Consider using a consent agenda to ensure adequate time for discussion. You may also want

Create a diverse board! Choose members with varied skills and knowledge to best support your organization and constituency needs.

QUICK TIP

to compile an organizational update, key background needed for decision-making points and highlights of the latest "good news."

DURING THE MEETING, STICK CLOSELY TO THE AGENDA TO MAKE GOOD USE OF EVERYONE'S TIME. Focus on getting results and critical decision-making at every meeting.

MAKE ATTENDANCE MANDATORY. Develop policies around meetings and hold members accountable. If a meeting is scheduled but agenda items have changed, don't waste members' time. Reschedule for another, more appropriate day.

ASK FOR BOARD INPUT ON THE AGENDA. This allows members to include topics of interest, increasing the likelihood of attendance, and helping to keep them engaged while there. This can also help the executive director better understand where members stand on important issues.

Use each meeting as a board development opportunity. Do a quick assessment at the end of the meeting and integrate improvements at the next meeting.

EXECUTIVE DIRECTORS AND FOUNDERS AS MEMBERS

While an executive director is often a member of the board, involved in board discussions and information sharing, he or she is rarely granted a vote. After all, the board is technically the executive director's employer and conflicts of interest could arise. To guard against this, both the board and the executive director should act independently from each other — the executive director as leader of the organization and the board in a governance role. Because of their passion and commitment, founders may want to directly exert their influence over the organization as a member of the board. Ultimately, the answer to this question rests in the board's confidence in the founder's ability to use his or her judgement to move the organization's mission forward at the governance level. As a board member, a founder can be granted a vote. This means he or she should be able to effectively address the organization's needs and provide guidance and support.

TERM LIMITS

Term limits give both the board member and the organization an opportunity to determine if continued service is in the best interest of both parties. To ensure the organization's ability to bring in fresh perspectives and expertise and foster its ability to be flexible and

BOARD ORIENTATION IS KEY!

▶ Develop an orientation manual outlining what each member needs to know about their board commitment and your organization.

▶ Give your board the tools they need to excel. Regularly update members on key organizational issues and good works.

▶ Use mentoring and ongoing education to help members feel prepared and informed.

Learn more!
Getting On Board with Effective Orientation (www.boardsource.org). This BoardSource Toolkit can help you design your board orientation materials and training sessions.

responsive to changing needs, many nonprofits set defined terms for their board members. These typically range from one to four years. However, some nonprofits choose not to adopt a limit — typically when an organization will benefit from the continued involvement of strong, active members. When developing policy in this area, think carefully about the needs of your organization.

BOARD COMMITTEES

Board committees help optimize individual expertise and diversity by allowing the board to focus resources more effectively. By operating in smaller groups, with distinctive responsibilities, members can often accomplish more. Board committees are also a great way to engage board members to volunteer in a meaningful way.

Certain types of committees may be required by law. In California, for example, charities with gross revenues exceeding $2 million must establish an audit committee.

BOARD ORIENTATION

Board orientation is critical to getting organization-wide buy-in to your mission, values, organizational identity and strategic plans. It helps improve communication and participation, defines expectations and empowers new members with the tools they need to steward your nonprofit in the community. Orientation prepares your board members to provide informed guidance and support in governance issues, allowing your organization to make better use of their expertise.

EXECUTIVE DIRECTOR EVALUATIONS

Executive director evaluations are a significant component of a board's responsibilities. They are critical to ensuring the executive director is in sync with a board and driving the organization forward toward its mission. Evaluations also help to clarify expectations and set goals for the future.

For more information about executive director evaluations, read Chapter 9: Managing People.

Use board committees to optimize individual expertise and use resources as effectively as possible.

QUICK TIP

Q | Where do we find board members?

A Finding the right candidates for your board is not an easy task. Ideally, you'll recruit individuals with a range of complementary skills who are as passionate about your mission as you are. So, where do you start?

First, think about the skills that will benefit your organization. There are often three key areas represented on the board:

- One-third would be individuals who have access to financial resources or soliciting donations.

- One-third would be individuals with management expertise in areas of financial, marketing, legal and the like.

- One-third would be individuals connected at the community level, with expertise in your service field.

Then, think about other characteristics such as age, gender, diversity, geographic representation and familiarity with your cause.

Consider current volunteers and significant donors as candidates. Ask for board and staff suggestions, and look at business leaders and high net-worth individuals in the community.

Sites like boardnetUSA (www.boardnetusa.org), VolunteerMatch (www.volunteermatch.org) and BoardSource (www.boardsource.org) also help nonprofit boards and new leaders find each other. The latter also offers "Recruiting a Stronger Board: A BoardSource Toolkit," which, among other tools, provides a sample board matrix to help you outline the desired expertise, sectors and demographics that comprise your board.

You might consider designating a board nominations committee to identify potential candidates. Ask the board to seek out candidates who can contribute in a unique way. And be sure to review each candidate in light of your mission and goals.

▶ Before you choose a board candidate, define and present board requirements for service, such as personal financial contributions, fundraising minimums, board meeting attendance, committee participation and the like. Be sure new board members are aware of the expectations before accepting the position.

Visit www.nonprofitanswerguide.org for timely sector resources and more expert answers to your most immediate nonprofit questions.

QUICK TIP

No. **5**

Q What role does the board chair play? What is his or her relationship with the executive director?

A Successful, mission-driven nonprofits have two things in common: 1. **A STRONG EXECUTIVE DIRECTOR** and 2. **AN ENGAGED, COLLABORATIVE BOARD CHAIR.** Without exception, the role of board chair is paramount to ensuring an active, focused and supportive board. This in turn ensures a healthy, effective nonprofit.

IMPORTANT WAYS THE BOARD CHAIR AND THE EXECUTIVE DIRECTOR WORK TOGETHER:

▶ Partnering to make sure board resolutions are carried out.

▶ Appointing committee chairs and recommending who will serve on committees.

▶ Preparing strategic agendas for board meetings that are geared toward thoughtful discussion and group decision-making.

▶ Conducting new board member orientation.

▶ Each acting as spokespersons when necessary.

The board chair's commitment to stakeholders is to operate under the guiding principle of what is best for the organization. He or she should facilitate board leadership and good governance. In this way, the chair molds the board's culture, work and impact.

A board chair is responsible for leading the board and setting the tone for all members. He or she oversees governance and policy setting, with a focus on mission, direction, priorities and evaluation. The chair has a significant influence on how the board uses its time (and in particular is often instrumental in helping the board address fundraising and strategic goals).

In addition to overseeing board and committee meetings, supporting recruitment and assessing the performance of board members and the executive director, the board chair works closely with the executive director. The two should meet regularly to collaboratively drive the organization's mission forward.

The working relationship between the executive director and board chair is key. Trust, respect and a willingness to rely on each other's strengths are critical, along with a common understanding of the organization's goals and the strategies needed to get there. Both the executive director and the chair should also have clearly defined roles and responsibilities so that everyone understands where one individual's authority ends and the other person's begins. This helps to determine what issues are matters for the board, and what issues lie in the domain of the organization itself.

Adapted in part from *BoardSource and the Board Chair Handbook, Second Edition* (www.boardsource.org).

Q How do we get board members engaged for our cause? How do we get them to raise funds?

A Board members play a vital role in helping an organization drive its mission forward. And in most instances, board members want to fulfill their responsibilities and contribute positively to the work of the nonprofit they serve. When a member is not actively participating, it's often due to a lack of understanding of what is expected or not having access to the tools necessary to participate effectively.

Actively involve your board in the development of strategic plans, including fundraising plans. A board can be a significant resource in terms of making introductions. In fact, they often have the business expertise that can be useful in developing a sound plan.

The board is responsible for ensuring the financial health of your organization. Getting them involved at the planning stage helps boards understand their fundraising responsibilities, builds excitement toward implementation and increases the likelihood that members will want to engage in actionable activities.

Ask each board member to annually make a specific giving and fundraising commitment. This process will clarify each member's role and inform the annual organizational planning for the year ahead. If you sense resistance, you may want to conduct a session with the board to discuss any reluctance to being involved in fundraising. Such a session may reveal the source of hesitation so you can address it.

Providing the board with outside training in fundraising strategies and techniques will help mitigate such fears, as will setting up a structure for successful fundraising that may include partnering board members with other board members, volunteers or staff members.

▶ Clear and consistent communication is key to fostering a fully engaged board. Consider hosting a retreat to talk about expectations and any challenges they've encountered as ambassadors of your mission and, if necessary, invest in board training to build their capacity.

Fundraising is an important responsibility for any board, but some members may be better suited to contributing in other ways, such as financial oversight, communications or introductions to strategic partners.

QUICK TIP

TIPS TO GET MEMBERS MOVING.

Gail Perry, the author of *Fired Up Fundraising: Turn Board Passion into Action*, suggests the following four steps:

1. Work with the board chair to get your board members involved in developing an annual fundraising plan. Put numbers on your program objectives, such as how many kids you'll send to camp or how many meals you want to serve to a needy public.

2. Communicate the community impact of the results of your efforts. Talk to your board about benefits in real terms, such as "We'll help kids who go to camp be healthier, have better self-esteem and do better in school." Or "We will help hungry people get nutritious meals right here in our community."

3. Create an action plan and give each board member a job. Ensure all individuals understand their role and how it relates to achieving results. How is each board member going to help make the plan a reality? For example, some may seek out sponsors, some may enlist volunteers and some may serve on committees to strengthen community and government relationships. Be sure to tie all responsibilities back to your cause and your fundraising goal.

4. Communicate regularly with your board members to keep excitement up and momentum going. Keep in touch weekly or monthly and keep them informed of your success. Board engagement is strongest when members' interests match those of the organization.

To learn more about getting your board engaged for your mission, read Chapter 5: Fundraising, and Chapter 6: Marketing and Communications.

Never doubt that a small group of thoughtful, concerned citizens can change world. Indeed it is the only thing that ever has.

- Margaret Mead

Q } How do we keep the board communicating effectively?

A } The board assumes a unique responsibility in the nonprofit sector. It is obligated to hire the executive director, develop policy, assume fiduciary responsibilities and support the executive director in implementing strategies to move the organization forward. Each member offers a diverse perspective, distinct expertise and unique character, yet all work toward a common goal.

Communication between the board and the executive director is vital to the health of your organization. Regular, open meetings between the board chair and the executive director are paramount and must be guided by what's best for the organization. Each should keep the other informed about trends, developments and relevant changes.

Disagreements should be respectfully resolved and areas of responsibility should be clear. As leaders in their respective positions, the executive director and the chair act as partners to guide your nonprofit and set the tone for the board and the organization at large.

TO KEEP THE BOARD COMMUNICATING AT ITS BEST, CONSIDER THE FOLLOWING:

FOCUS MEETINGS ON STRATEGY, NOT JUST ADMINISTRATION. A consent agenda makes it easy for routine issues to be dispensed with quickly. Then, get your board talking about deeper issues that can help you meet your goals. Provide clear, concise agendas and disseminate them in advance so board members can come prepared to engage, ask insightful questions and provide informed opinions.

INVITE CANDID DISCUSSIONS. Create an environment that encourages board members to freely express their opinions, even if they challenge the status quo. Consider bringing in a facilitator to discuss complex issues. This will help keep the chair, executive director or any one member from pushing a particular agenda in an attempt to sway the group.

IF YOUR BOARD IS LARGE, CONSIDER BREAKING UP INTO GROUPS FOR DISCUSSION. Smaller group discussions encourage creativity and may provide an opportunity for less outspoken members to join in and offer their expertise.

MAKE IT EASY FOR THE BOARD TO UNDERSTAND AND ACT. Use real examples and frame issues in terms of what you want the board to do. Discuss strategies you want to implement and talk about how you intend to get there.

> ▶ Remember, the chair and the executive director set the tone for effective communications organization-wide. If they're not working together to resolve issues and act in a unified manner in the best interest of the organization, neither will the board.

Q | What are bylaws and why do we need them? How can they protect the board?

A › Bylaws are the written rules by which an organization is governed. They set forth the structure of the board and the organization. They determine the rights of participants and they determine the procedures by which rights can be exercised. In other words, bylaws guide the board in conducting business. Carefully crafted bylaws and adherence to them can help ensure the fairness of board decisions and provide protection against legal challenges.

It's important to note that bylaws are in fact legal documents. This means there are legal requirements for what should be included. These requirements vary depending on the state in which you operate. For example, some state laws require membership, board selection and other issues to be stated in the articles of incorporation. To be sure your bylaws are on side with state laws, consult a lawyer before you begin.

Adapted in part from *The Nonprofit Board's Guide to Bylaws*, by D. Benson Tesdahl (BoardSource, 2003).

Bylaws can help protect your directors and officers from personal liability. For example, your nonprofit can protect its directors and officers from costs arising from wrongful lawsuits by including provisions regarding indemnification in your bylaws.

In some cases, nonprofits are required to indemnify directors and officers, that is, protect and defend them from loss or harm resulting from risk. In other cases, they are prohibited from doing so. (In California, see California codes 5238 and 9246 for more details.)

Here's an example: A nonprofit is required to indemnify a director or officer for all costs the director incurred in successfully defending himself against a lawsuit. In such a case, issues could arise regarding the nonprofit's ability to advance funds to the director to pay for defense, or its ability to reimburse the director for losses as required by law. For this reason, insurance is necessary. This topic is discussed in more detail in Chapter 2: Legal.

Purchasing Directors and Officers Liability Insurance (D&O Insurance) will enable your nonprofit to indemnify your directors and officers. And, in the case of nonprofits that have enough assets to indemnify directors and officers out of the nonprofit's funds, insurance will reimburse your nonprofit for funds advanced for legal defense.

▶ State and local laws surrounding governing documents are complex and varied. To ensure you fully understand your rights and responsibilities, and ensure the bylaws you develop are in compliance with all applicable laws, you should consult a lawyer who understands nonprofit tax-exempt organizations.

D&O Insurance can also pay for losses incurred against, which the nonprofit is not permitted by statute to indemnify.

In fact, if your nonprofit is not able to offer this protection you may run the risk of being unable to recruit qualified directors.

Before you sign on the dotted line, consider having your attorney or nonprofit insurance specialist explain your policy in detail.

BE SURE TO ASK:

- Does the policy automatically cover directors and officers who come on after the policy has taken effect?
- Does the policy provide for the advancement of funds to pay defense costs as they come due?
- Is there coverage for claims arising from events occurring before the beginning of the policy period?
- Does the policy provide coverage for employment practices liability?
- What are the limits and deductibles?

D&O INSURANCE DOES TWO THINGS:

▶ It directly reimburses directors for legal costs they incur, which the nonprofit cannot or will not pay.

▶ It reimburses the nonprofit for the costs it incurs in indemnifying directors.

" Safety is a cheap and effective insurance policy. "

- Author Unknown

Carefully crafted bylaws help ensure the fairness of board decisions and provide protection against legal challenges, protecting your directors and officers from personal liability.

QUICK TIP

Q | How do you deal with an ineffective board member?

A } Most individuals choose to serve on a board because they want to contribute their expertise, collaborate with peers, give back to the community and affect change in a meaningful way. However, there are instances in which a board member is not effectively engaged, or is ineffective in his or her role. There may be a reasonable explanation. When addressing the "why," consider the following barriers:

1. The board member is not clear on what is expected.

2. The board member is not comfortable with an assignment given.

3. The board member has served for too long. He or she has lost commitment or is "burnt out."

4. The board member is not in the right role. He or she really wants to be a direct service volunteer.

5. The board member may have too many competing demands and is not as available right now to serve as an active volunteer.

▶ Involving the board in developing and maintaining up-to-date "job descriptions" for your board members, board chair and committee members can go a long way toward helping them to understand what's expected of them.

Whatever the case, you'll want the board chair to resolve the problem right away. He or she should meet with the member to discuss what is causing reduced participation and seek an appropriate resolution. Clarifying expectations and providing training, orientation or coaching may help the member meet expectations. If the case is that the member is "burnt out," or over extended, allowing him or her to gracefully resign may be the appropriate solution.

To help mitigate the chance of a member becoming ineffective, develop expectations in writing. Provide them to each potential board member before they accept the position. Once on board, orient individuals to ensure your organization's mission, goals and objectives are clearly understood. Along the way, keep your board updated on your good work and get members involved where appropriate. Consider starting formal committees to put boundaries on responsibilities and tasks. And don't forget to conduct annual board evaluations to determine what's working and what isn't.

Q How important is board assessment? What are the steps in board evaluation?

A Performance evaluations are often a cause for apprehension, even among board members. Individuals tend to assume a performance assessment is designed to highlight bad performance, but this should not be the case. Without review and reflection, it's impossible to determine whether your board and your organization are meeting goals and making progress.

BOARD EVALUATIONS ARE DESIGNED TO DO THE FOLLOWING:

IDENTIFY GAPS AND IMPROVE PERFORMANCE. They help the chair and the executive director understand where they may need to support board members with training, coaching or mentoring to help a member meet goals and objectives.

HOLD THE BOARD ACCOUNTABLE FOR ITS PERFORMANCE. They create transparency and add credibility to board decision-making.

OFFER AN OPPORTUNITY TO COMMUNICATE OBJECTIVELY. They offer a vehicle to openly discuss strengths and weaknesses and realign board members with the organization's identity, mission, values and goals.

FOR THE CHAIR, PROVIDE IMPORTANT FEEDBACK ON LEADERSHIP STYLE AND FACILITATION SKILLS. They highlight the chair's strengths and weaknesses in handling challenges, and his or her ability to keep board members engaged.

To get started, experts recommend a nonprofit board conduct a self-assessment every two years. That said, it's also important to assess each board member's performance before a new term is granted.

Individual board members' performance can be tied to a full board assessment process by asking board members to rate their own performance at the same time that they rate board performance. You may also want board members to conduct peer evaluations, and assess other board members' contributions.

Boards should conduct a self-assessment every two years and each individual board member's performance should be assessed before a new term is granted.

QUICK TIP

No. 10

Board chair performance can be evaluated by the governance committee or you may want to ask board members to provide anonymous assessments. The results should be communicated in a private meeting.

TO MAKE EVALUATIONS WORK MOST EFFECTIVELY, CONSIDER THE FOLLOWING:

GET BOARD BUY-IN. Without consensus from all members, the board won't participate.

RESEARCH AND EXPLORE BEFORE YOU JUMP IN. If you're new to board assessment, form a task force to investigate how to appropriately conduct a self-assessment. Research the self-assessment tools available and choose those that are best aligned with your needs. Get board members involved at the research and selection phase and have them refine their chosen tool for effective self-reflection. If costs are a concern, identify foundations that fund board development activities and include assessment costs in the organization's budget.

DEVOTE TIME TO PLANNING. Ensure members have enough time to complete the assessment and determine when and how you'll discuss results.

CONSIDER BRINGING IN A FACILITATOR. Members need to know how to give constructive feedback. If anyone is unclear, you may want to bring in a facilitator to aid in the evaluation process and help discussions go smoothly.

FOLLOW UP AND IMPLEMENT RECOMMENDATIONS TO AFFECT REAL BOARD CHANGE. Expectations and duties should be clarified and each member should be provided with opportunities for self-improvement.

Adapted in part from *BoardSource, Assessing your Performance* (www.boardsource.org/Spotlight.asp?ID=14.530).

To be effective, evaluations require board buy-in, a well-developed assessment process and follow-up to provide opportunities for self-improvement.

QUICK TIP

KNOWLEDGE CENTERS

- **BoardSource**
  (www.boardsource.org)
- **Blue Avocado**
  (www.blueavocado.org)
- **The Center on Philanthropy
  at Indiana University**
  (www.philanthropy.iupui.edu)
- **Free Management Library**
  (www.managementhelp.org/boards)
- **Nonprofit and Philanthropy
  Good Practice**
  (www.npgoodpractice.org)
- **Stanford Social Innovation Review**
  (www.ssireview.org)

BOARD RECRUITMENT

- **Riordan Volunteer Leadership
  Development Program**
  (www.rvldp.org)
- **boardnetUSA**
  (www.boardnetusa.org)
- **VolunteerMatch**
  (www.volunteermatch.org)
- **Volunteer.org**

BOOKS

- *The Board Book: An Insider's Guide
  for Directors and Trustees,*
  by William Bowen
- *Extraordinary Board Leadership:
  The Keys to High-Impact Governing,*
  by Doug Eadie
- *Good Governance for Nonprofits:
  Developing Principles and Policies
  for an Effective Board,* by Frederic L.
  Laughlin and Robert Andringa
- *Great Boards for Small Groups:
  A 1-Hour Guide to Governing a
  Growing Nonprofit,* by Andy Robinson
- *The Ultimate Board Member's Book,*
  by Kay Sprinkel Grace

READY-TO-GO-RESOURCES

20-SECOND-SUMMARY

FOR THE BOARD CHAIR

- Be flexible. Seek out what motivates your board and tap into it. Don't be afraid to use "big issues" to get boards to rise to the occasion.

- Be a champion for your organization. Trust your instincts and be rigorous in approach, assessment and review.

FOR THE EXECUTIVE DIRECTOR

- Remember you and the board chair are a team. Clearly define roles and responsibilities, keep communication open and commit to resolving disagreements respectfully.

- Start strong. Ensure everyone understands the organization's identity, value, mission and goals. Insist on board member orientations.

- Bring all of your strategic thinking, communication and management skills to the table. You're going to need them.

Sound financial management is one of the biggest keys to success for any nonprofit organization.

Your needs will vary considerably based on the size of your organization, scope of your mission and sources of income.

That said, two things never change: Whether you have one employee or one thousand, your organization will need accurate bookkeeping and committed, credible oversight. With those in place, you'll be in a better position to maintain your 501(c)(3) status, raise and manage necessary funds and protect the resources needed to deliver on your mission.

This chapter is designed to guide you through an overview of key accounting indicators and functions as they relate to nonprofits. We also outline important regulatory, governance and tax considerations. Even if numbers aren't your thing, the topics discussed in this chapter should give you a good sense of the areas to explore with your bookkeeper, accountant and board.

DISCLAIMER:
The information contained in this book is general in nature and may not be applicable to all situations. In addition, laws change. You should refer to the most current editions of additional resources listed for each topic and consult with an attorney or accountant on important matters.

Q | What are the financial benchmarks for a healthy nonprofit?

A | There are no magic rules that apply to all nonprofits. Type and size of organization, sources of revenue and the length of time your organization has existed are just a few of the factors to consider. That said, there are several common measures that can be helpful in assessing the financial health of your nonprofit organization:

- **THE QUICK RATIO** ([current assets - inventories]/current liabilities) indicates your organization's ability to meet short-term obligations. As a general guideline, a quick ratio of 1 or more is good.

- **THE DEBT RATIO** (total debt/total assets) indicates the proportion of debt relative to assets. A high value can suggest liquidity problems and, just as it would for an individual, may be perceived as a risk by creditors. A debt ratio of 1 or less is good.

- **THE DEFENSIVE INTERVAL RATIO** ([cash + marketable securities]/ [operational expenses/365]) measures the number of days an organization can operate without having to tap into long-term (fixed) assets. This lets you know how long your cash reserves will last. Most experts recommend maintaining enough cash on hand to cover three to six months of operating expenses. See question 10 for more on this topic.

It should be noted that in addition to standard financial analysis, an examination of your organization's sources of revenue (e.g., grants, individual donations, fees for service, etc.) relative to total revenue can also be useful. This will help to identify opportunities to diversify revenue streams and assess potential areas of risk, such as if a large portion of funding is coming from only one source.

▶ Financial ratios can be very useful in determining the financial health of your organization. While you'll want to become familiar with the full range of measures available, start with the basics: quick, debt and defensive interval ratios will give you a good snapshot of your finances.

QUICK TIP

A qualified bookkeeper or accountant should be able to provide you with the ongoing financial analysis necessary to regularly assess the financial health of your nonprofit and keep up with current accounting requirements.

No. **2**

Q | How should a nonprofit prepare its budget? What steps are involved and what role does the board play?

A | Your operational budget is the foundation from which all of your work will be carried out. It allows you to establish benchmarks, gauge financial health from one year to the next and determine priorities.

HERE ARE SOME KEY STEPS IN DEVELOPING YOUR BUDGET:

- Establish your budget period (one year, multiple years).

- Review program achievements and financial performance for the prior year.

- Set program and organizational goals for your budget period.

- **ESTIMATE EXPENSES, INCLUDING:**

  1. Fixed costs such as staff, rent, taxes, utilities, etc.

  2. Variable costs that fluctuate based on activity level (e.g., the cost to vaccinate more clients in a health clinic would fluctuate based on the number of clients and environmental factors such as a flu outbreak).

  3. Incremental expenses, which occur when a particular action is taken (e.g., when a certain amount of money is raised, a new program will be launched).

- Estimate anticipated revenue.

- Plan for needed cash flow and development of cash reserves.

- Adjust to align expenses and revenue.

Your board of directors should be called upon to comment on and approve your organization's budget each year. From there, it becomes a tool for monitoring progress and determining areas for refinement, if necessary. Your budget should also be provided to the board at least quarterly, along with comparisons to the prior quarter and prior year and projections for the remainder of the year.

Adapted in part from *Finance Manual*, by Jan Masaoka and Jude Kaye.

> When it comes to planning your budget, be conservative. It's easy to say how much money you'd like to raise, but it's far more important to be practical about what can be raised. That way you'll be setting realistic goals for your staff and managing everyone's expectations, including your own.

Get the board involved! Your board of directors should comment on and approve your organization's budget each year.

QUICK TIP

Q | What are the major differences between nonprofit and for-profit accounting?

A | While many aspects of nonprofit and for-profit business accounting are similar (such as the tracking and reporting of income and expenses and payroll taxes), there are significant differences. These arise out of the nonprofit organization's duty to drive its resources toward its mission. For example, nonprofits are required to itemize expenses across management (general and administrative), fundraising and program areas. These are called "functional expenses" and the IRS requires that they be reported.

The requirement for nonprofits to report functional expenses also highlights the importance of a cost allocation plan. This basically means establishing a system that defines how you will allocate expenses across the various functional areas and to specific programs. For example, let's say that those involved in administrative functions take up 20 percent of your office space. You might then allocate 20 percent of an expense like paper to the administrative functional area.

A cost allocation plan can be extremely useful in determining how much a program or activity actually costs and, done accurately, it gives a clearer picture of the organization's finances. There are several acceptable methods — such as applying direct/indirect costs, and allocations based on percentage of payroll or physical space used (as in the example above). Frequently, a combination of these methods will be appropriate. Consult with your accountant to determine the approach that best suits your organization.

Other key aspects of interest to nonprofits are outlined by the Financial Accounting Standards Board (FASB), a nonprofit organization authorized by the Securities and Exchange Commission to set accounting standards in the United States. Of particular importance is the FASB's Statement of Financial Accounting Standards No.116, which defines:

- **REVENUE IN THE FORM OF CONTRIBUTIONS:** These standards establish how and when to recognize that revenue has been earned. They include standards for the accounting treatment of unrestricted and restricted funds, donated goods, in-kind contributions, pledges and the like.

▷ Unlike corporations, nonprofits are required to itemize and report "functional expenses." Generally, these are management (general and administrative), fundraising and program area expenses.

No. 3

VALUE OF DONATED SERVICES: This establishes standards for when it is necessary to record donated services (i.e., volunteer time) in the organization's financial statements. According to the FASB, services to be recognized include those that "(a) create or enhance nonfinancial assets or (b) require specialized skills, are provided by individuals possessing those skills and would typically need to be purchased if not provided by donation."

Another area that's important to nonprofits, while rarely affecting for-profits, is the reporting of restricted contributions. While the amounts of restricted contributions are reported on a nonprofit's 990 tax return, donors will typically require much greater detail about the use of restricted funds. This serves to inform the donor that the conditions of the gift have been (or are being) met, and enables staff to track what funds remain available for the restricted purpose.

A for-profit has a duty to its investors and customers. A nonprofit has a duty to its mission and clients. That means some parts of accounting will be the same and others will be vastly different.

❝ *You give but little when you give of your possessions. It is when you give of yourself that you truly give.* **❞**

- Kahlil Gibran, Author

Visit www.nonprofitanswerguide.org **for timely sector resources and more expert answers to your most immediate nonprofit questions.**

QUICK TIP

Q What are the basic financial reports that a nonprofit must prepare?

A The basic financial reports of a nonprofit organization include:

- **STATEMENT OF FINANCIAL POSITION** (also called a balance sheet): This summarizes the assets, liabilities and net assets of the organization at a specified date. It's a snapshot of the organization's financial position on that date.

- **STATEMENT OF ACTIVITY** (also called an income and expense statement): This reports the organization's financial activity over a period of time. It shows income minus expenses, which results in either a profit or a loss.

- **STATEMENT OF CASH FLOW:** This summarizes the resources that become available to the organization during the reporting period and the uses made of such resources. It's useful in real-time because it reports income received and expenses paid. A statement of projected cash flow can help the board and organization to be able to anticipate any shortfalls for planning purposes.

- **STATEMENT OF FUNCTIONAL EXPENSES:** Reports all expenses as related either to program services or to supporting services. Expenses under program services are shown divided among the various programs. Expenses under supporting services are generally divided between (1) management and general expenses and (2) fundraising expenses.

While these reports are extremely important in terms of understanding your organization's financial health and conveying that information to your board, you'll also find that these types of reports will often be required by funders when applying for grants.

Other reports, depending on your organization's needs, are: government information returns, payroll tax returns, reports to funders, management reports, budget monitoring reports and analysis of statements and investment reports.

A detailed list of financial reports for nonprofits, can be found in *Financial Statements of Not-for-Profit Organizations*, by the Financial Accounting Standards Board (www.fasb.org).

There are also a few accounting basics you should keep in mind. A qualified bookkeeper can help you to ensure reports are prepared properly and in a timely manner. He or she can also help to reconcile bank statements on a monthly basis, which is critical, and lend support and key information during budget development.

▶ A qualified bookkeeper can assist with day-to-day financial activities, monthly bank reconciliations, filing of payroll taxes and preparation of financial reports. In addition, a CPA can assist with preparation of tax documents and filing of IRS Form 990.

No. **5**

Q } What about audits? Does a
nonprofit need to have one? What
kinds are there?

A } At its best, the term "audit" usually sparks apprehension.
While it can refer to contract monitoring, internal review or
external management review, a lot of people think immediately of an
IRS review.

In actuality, a financial audit most commonly refers to an
independent review of an organization's financial books. Usually
conducted annually, it's really just a part of a reliable checks-and-
balances system to make sure everything is in order. Here, we
address whether a nonprofit needs an audit or other independent
review of its financial condition.

First, it's important to know if an annual financial audit is required
of your organization by the federal government or by your state. These
standards vary considerably. The federal government requires any
organization receiving federal funds of more than $500,000 in a year
to undergo a "Single Audit," which generally covers the year/program
in question.

State governments typically regulate the independent-audit
requirement based on income — whatever the source. For example,
in Pennsylvania, nonprofits that receive more than $300,000 in
funds must file an audited financial statement with the Department
of Revenue. In California, gross receipts totaling more than $2
million carry a similar requirement. Some states require an audited
statement simply by virtue of fundraising there, regardless of where
an organization's headquarters may be located.

Given these variations, it's best to consult an experienced attorney or
accountant to determine the specific needs of your organization.

Another factor to consider is the requirements of funding sources. In
addition to the requirements of federal and state governments, some
funders may require an independent audit as a condition of funding.

If you and your board do determine that an audit is beneficial
(or required), it's important to know that it must be prepared by

**Federal and state audit standards vary, so consult an experienced attorney or
accountant to determine the specific needs of your organization.**

QUICK TIP

a licensed independent certified public accountant (CPA). Once engaged, an auditor performs a series of selective tests that provide a basis for judging whether the financial reports can be relied upon.

Auditors will examine, among other things, bank reconciliations, selected restricted donations (to see that they were handled and recorded properly) and grant letters (to see that receivables are accurately stated). In addition, the auditor reviews physical assets, journals, ledgers and board minutes. Based on this investigation, the auditor issues a formal opinion about the accuracy of the financial reports.

If you do undergo an audit, you'll also want to establish an audit committee within your board of directors. These committees are typically responsible for selecting (or approving the selection of) an auditor, reviewing the auditor's outputs and meeting with the auditor pre- and post-audit to address any issues or questions. Audit committees also frequently have ongoing responsibility for the organization's overall financial oversight and internal financial controls.

No. 5

▶ Make sure you're up to speed on whether an audit is legally required. The federal government requires any organization receiving federal funds of more than $500,000 in a year to undergo an audit. States have their own regulations, usually based on a nonprofit's income – whatever the source. Funders may also require it as a condition of funding.

" I don't think there's a company, a management, an audit committee that hasn't gone back and relooked at what they're doing. People are really scrutinizing and want to make sure their financial houses are in order. "

- William Esry, Former Chief Executive, Sprint Corporation

^{NO.}**6**

Q What are the tax and reporting requirements of nonprofits?

A All tax-exempt organizations must file certain reports with federal, state and local authorities. Because of distinctive state and local requirements, it's important that you consult with your legal counsel and accountant to ensure that the necessary paperwork is being filed for your organization. That said, at the federal level, you'll definitely need to file one of the following:

- Form 990, Return of Organization Exempt from Income Tax

- Form 990-EZ, Short Form Return of Organization Exempt from Income Tax

- 990-N (e-postcard) for exempt organizations that normally have less than $50,000 in gross receipts

See question 3 of Chapter 2: Legal, for more information regarding these forms and requirements in the state of California.

In terms of paying taxes, exempt organizations are exempt from income taxes, but they are still required to pay payroll taxes. Typically these are withheld from employee paychecks and paid quarterly. Be sure to file and pay on time. Willful failure to pay is a felony under federal law and the interest and penalties for late filing can add up quickly.

The IRS provides an Exempt Employer's Toolkit (www.irs.gov/charities/article/0,,id=172794,00.html), which includes all of the forms that must be filed by organizations that have employees.

In addition to federal requirements, you'll need to file payroll taxes with your state and, in some cases, locally. Check with your state's Department of Revenue to determine when and where to file payroll taxes.

Another factor to consider at the state and local level is the need to collect sales tax. If you engage in the sale of taxable goods and services, you may have to collect and remit sales tax. Check with the Department of Revenue in your state to determine whether this applies to you and, if so, the required process.

▷ There is no excuse for failing to remit payroll taxes on time. Willful failure to pay is a felony under federal law and the interest and penalties for late filing can add up quickly.

Check out IRS.gov and search for "Charities" to find out what's required of nonprofit organizations.

QUICK TIP

Q | What internal financial controls are recommended? What does the Sarbanes–Oxley Act have to do with it?

A An independent audit (see question 5) is one form of internal financial control, but it's important to put ongoing procedures into place as well. This helps to safeguard an organization's assets and enhance reliability of its financial records. Internal controls provide assurance that transactions are properly authorized and recorded, accountability over assets is maintained, and access to assets is limited to authorized individuals.

In 2002, the federal government passed the American Competitiveness and Corporate Accountability Act (a.k.a. the Sarbanes-Oxley Act). This Act compels corporate boards to monitor and be responsible for their companies' financial transactions and audit procedures. That is, it regulates their financial controls.

Why does this matter to you? The Act itself doesn't apply to nonprofits, but there are a number of provisions that you might consider voluntarily adopting, particularly as they relate to board oversight and committees, disclosure, document retention and audits.

Another reason this Act may be relevant to your nonprofit is that it inspired a number of state laws that do apply to nonprofits, such as the California Nonprofit Integrity Act of 2004 which addresses registration of a charity, financial reporting, auditing and other areas relevant to a nonprofit's finances and management.

In addition to familiarizing yourself with state laws, following are a few areas to consider as you develop your internal controls:

- Organizational budget, size and objectives

- Board and staff involvement in finances

- Establishment of audit and/or finance committees

- Organizational structure and governance

- Segregation of duties

- Recordkeeping and recording systems

- Authorization protocols

- Periodic board review

- Cost-benefit analysis (e.g., is the cost of the proposed system aligned with the benefits of implementation for your particular organization?)

NO.
8

Q } **What is an investment policy?
When is it advisable to have one
and why is it important?**

A } Any organization that invests assets should have an
investment policy. This is a document that outlines your
overall strategy for investing, your short- and long-term goals and
the process by which investment decisions are made.

The board of directors needs to make two critical decisions in regard
to investment policies: asset allocation (or, diversification) and
spending parameters. These decisions will provide insights into an
organization's investment practices, its historical return, its asset
allocation and its compliance with the Uniform Prudent Management
of Institutional Funds Act (UPMIFA).

Following, you'll find a list of questions the board of directors should
answer in setting investment policies for your organization:

- Does your organization have an investment policy statement?
  If so, when was it last updated? Does it meet your objectives and
  needs? Is it consistent with the UPMIFA and state law?

- What is your return goal over the period of your plan?

- What is your current spending rate (percentage of endowment
  transferred to operating fund)?

- What is your projected contribution level and liquidity needs?

- From whom has the organization received endowments, grants
  and contributions?

- Is there a board committee responsible for investments?
  How often does it meet and report to full board?

- How do you currently monitor investment performance?

- Have you evaluated the cost of your investment managers?

- What is your current asset allocation in the portfolio?

- What are the organization's attitudes toward risk and returns
  within the portfolio?

- Are your investments subject to any unusual regulations?

- Have you adopted a policy regarding investments in companies
  that may conflict with your mission?

- Has the organization transferred cash and investments to any
  related organizations?

- Who manages the portfolio and are any unique skills required?

Q | What has changed with the new 990?

A The 990 is the primary federal return for tax-exempt organizations. In 2008, the IRS released its first major revision in more than 20 years. The reason, according to the IRS, is that the old form "failed to reflect the changes in the law and the increasing size, diversity and complexity of the exempt sector."

While there are changes to most tax forms every year, when you hear about the "new 990," people are generally referring to the 2008 overhaul.

SO WHAT'S NEW? HERE'S A QUICK SUMMARY:

- The addition of a section on governance, including requests for information on the governing body, management practices and disclosure policies, such as in the case of a conflict of interest.

- Revisions to the way executive compensation is reported, along with transactions with "interested persons," such as board members and independent contractors.

- New definitions of officers, directors, trustees and key employees.

- The addition of thresholds and exceptions for organizations required to file certain reports. This is designed to reduce the reporting burden for many organizations.

- Revised filing amounts (i.e., gross receipts and assets) for organizations eligible to file the 990-EZ.

- The addition of an annual electronic filing requirement for tax-exempt organizations normally with annual gross receipts of less than $25,000. These organizations are not required to file a 990 or 990-EZ, but must file a Form 990-N, Electronic Notice (e-Postcard).

- Reduction of required attachments; addition of new schedules. Financial reporting, fundraising, gaming activities (such as a charity-run bingo game) and treatment of endowments and art collections are just a few of the items covered in the new schedules.

> In 2008, for the first time in nearly 20 years, the 990 underwent a massive overhaul. The changes were designed to reflect the needs and composition of a sector that had changed drastically over that time.

For a good summary of major changes to the 990, go to IRS.gov and search "overview of form 990 redesign."

QUICK TIP

NO.
10

Q | How can we move toward having a cash reserve fund?

A | Cash reserves (in this case, meaning cash on hand or more formally, "operating reserves") are critical for any organization. Most experts recommend maintaining enough cash on hand to cover three to six months of operating expenses. However, this is a generalization and may not apply to all organizations.

It's important to consider your own unique circumstances. For example, an organization that relies largely on fees for service or has long-term contracts in place may not need six months of reserves. For a newly launched organization, six months is likely unrealistic but could be an important goal. Whatever your nonprofit's situation, it's widely agreed that all organizations should have an absolute bare-minimum of one month's reserves.

Moving toward the development of a cash reserve fund is not unlike building up your own personal savings account. You need to look at where revenue is coming in, where it's allocated (for example, monies earmarked for rent or restricted donations won't be helpful here), and where it can be drawn upon to bolster cash reserves. Sometimes, you need to tighten your belt.

There are a few primary places from where a nonprofit can draw off funds to strengthen the cash reserve: fees for service, individual donations, general operating grants and fundraising events. As you develop your budget (see question 2), consider how much funding is coming from these or other relevant sources and begin to siphon off a percentage for your cash reserves. Establishing a benchmark, say 10 percent, can be helpful in prioritizing other areas of your budget in ways that can help meet that goal.

You won't get to six months' reserves overnight but progress can be made relatively quickly.

> Experts recommend three to six months of reserves depending on your situation. At a bare minimum, plan to have one month's operating expenses on hand. Just like your personal savings, with a careful look at how money is coming in and going out, progress can be made relatively quickly.

To create a cash reserve plan, look at receivables alongside projected cash flow and expenses. Be realistic about setting aside funds over time.

QUICK TIP

FINANCIAL MANAGEMENT

- *Financial Responsibilities of Nonprofit Boards, Second Edition,* by Andrew S. Lang for BoardSource

- *Nonprofit Integrity Act of 2004, Summary of Key Provisions:* www.ag.ca.gov/charities/publications/ nonprofit_integrity_act_nov04.pdf

- *The Sarbanes-Oxley Act and Implications for Nonprofit Organizations by BoardSource and Independent Sector:* www.boardsource.org/clientfiles/ Sarbanes-Oxley.pdf

- *Nonprofit Finance Fund:* www.nonprofitfinancefund.org

ACCOUNTING STANDARDS

- *Accounting for Contributions Received and Contributions Made,* by the Financial Accounting Standards Board: www.fasb.org/pdf/aop_FAS116.pdf

- *Financial Statements of Not-for-Profit Organizations,* by the Financial Accounting Standards Board: www.fasb.org/pdf/aop_FAS117.pdf

TAX RESOURCES

- *Compliance Guide for 501(c)(3) Public Charities,* Internal Revenue Service: www.irs.gov/pub/irs-pdf/p4221pc.pdf

- Employment Taxes for Exempt Organizations, IRS: www.irs.gov/charities/article/0,,id= 128716,00.html

- IRS Background Paper – Form 990, Moving from the Old to the New: www.irs.gov/pub/irs-tege/moving_from_ old_to_new.pdf

READY-TO-GO-RESOURCES

20-SECOND-SUMMARY

- Always file tax returns and remit payroll taxes on time. Willful failure to remit payroll taxes is a felony under federal law and the interest and penalties can add up quickly.

- Put internal control systems in place to ensure that your financial books are credible and accurate.

- If you aren't completely comfortable with bookkeeping and financial management, engage someone who is.

- There's no magic formula for financial health. Your needs and approach must be customized to the type, size and location of your organization. If you want to see how you stack up against others, look at similarly sized organizations with a related mission.

- Board members have a duty – and sometimes a legal responsibility – to provide oversight and direction on financial management. Be sure to review the numbers regularly.

5 FUNDRAISING

Fundraising is usually high on a nonprofit's priority list.

In fact, there's a good chance you turned to this chapter first. It makes sense. You're fully committed to your mission and the programs that advance it, but none of it comes free.

On top of that, there's intense competition for limited resources – a fact that's never been more apparent than during the economic downturn in recent years.

This chapter describes the various types of funding sources that you should be considering and provides guidance on developing a plan to reach them. There are lots of things to consider – the role of your board, a communications plan, an online presence and diversification, to name a few – so think of this as a springboard to taking your fundraising to the next level.

Q } What's different in this economy?

A } Nonprofits have been hit especially hard by the economic downturn in recent years. As foundation endowments shrunk alongside corporate, government and personal budgets, charitable contributions plummeted. The good news is, the latest reports show signs of a rebound.

According to the Nonprofit Research Collaborative 2010 Fundraising Survey, the number of nonprofits reporting decreased contributions dropped by 14 percentage points, while those reporting increased contributions grew by 13 percentage points. That's promising, but there's a long way left to go.

Nonprofits represent a trailing sector. That means they are typically the last to rebound because they rely on the liquidity of other sectors. Those with endowments have often had to draw from them during tough times. Worse yet, as personal wealth has decreased, the need for many of the services nonprofits provide has risen.

Economic circumstances have led many nonprofits to look at new options to use their resources more efficiently. Certainly budget cuts and staff reductions have been a reality but so have mergers. Many nonprofits are maximizing resources by joining forces organizationally, operationally (such as by sharing offices and administrative staff) or at the program level. Assuming strong mission alignment and a sound agreement between the organizations, this can be an extremely effective approach, particularly for smaller organizations.

Another trend that can emerge in a difficult economy (or, frankly, in any economic circumstance) is the concept of grant chasing. When funds are in short supply, it can be very tempting to pursue funding for programs that aren't tightly aligned with your mission. The problem – in addition to your legal responsibility to use funds for exempt purposes – is that it can easily get out of hand. Organizations can quickly find themselves spending time managing multiple programs that aren't aligned with their overall strategy.

THE BOTTOM LINE:

▶ Whatever the economic conditions, nonprofits can succeed with a commitment to planning, fiduciary responsibility and sound management.

No. **2**

Q What are the major types of fundraising sources?

A The types of fundraising most appropriate to your organization will depend on the nature of your work, your size and your geographical presence (e.g., a neighborhood vs. a national organization). The primary types of fundraising sources include the following:

- **HIGH-NET-WORTH INDIVIDUALS:** For many nonprofits, these individuals represent a significant portion of revenue. They are typically people who live in your community and have a personal commitment to your mission, and they must be cultivated in a very personal way. Companies like WealthEngine (www.wealthengine.com) can be very useful in identifying donors in your area. Your board plays a crucial role in developing and maintaining these relationships. In addition, a skilled director of development should be in a position to support this function by identifying and helping to steward donors.

- **THE PUBLIC:** According to *Giving USA 2011* by the Giving USA Foundation, individual contributions accounted for 73 percent of all charitable giving in 2010. In other words, cultivating a broad base of individual donors is critical to fundraising success. Typically these donations are considered unrestricted and are not tied to a specific program (whereas a grant might be), so the funds you raise can be applied to where they are most needed. Online giving, direct mail and events are common ways to engage individuals. The most important thing is to continue the relationship after the gift has been received.

- **SPECIAL EVENTS:** Events are a fundraising mainstay for many nonprofits. The most effective ones tend to feature fun, unique content; a clear target market; an event budget that ensures no more than 50 percent of the revenue will go to costs; and a committed volunteer base to help plan, organize and spread the word. Most importantly, truly impactful events feature a clear connection to the organization's mission and are hosted by an organization that connects with donors year-round.

A successful nonprofit will consider and target a full range of funding sources. As with an investment portfolio, diversity is key to long-term stability.

QUICK TIP

- **FOUNDATION GRANTS:** Philanthropic funding can be an important part of fundraising, particularly as it relates to funding specific programs, events or capital campaigns. If you're new to this type of funding, it's important to set realistic expectations. Foundations of all sizes are inundated with requests and can usually only fund a small percentage of the proposals they receive. Relationships are as important here as they are with individual donors. Keep in mind that these funders will respond best when they see evidence of community support, including from your own board.

  If you represent a small, local organization, start out by seeking grants from small community foundations in your area. Foundation Directory Online (www. fconline.foundationcenter.org) offers subscription-based services to research foundations of all sizes. You might also consider signing up for RFP alerts from Philanthropy News Digest. The Center for Nonprofit Management also offers a list of fundraising databases that will be useful to you. For more information, visit www.cnmsocal.org/category/fundraising-and-marketing.html.

- **GOVERNMENT FUNDING:** Government grants cover a wide range of areas, from the arts and education to community development and technology. A great way to identify and apply for federal funding is through www.grants.gov, a clearinghouse of grants from numerous public agencies. For state and local grants, a search of agency websites can be useful, as can low-cost subscription services such as www.findrfp.com. It's important to note that government funders are typically the least flexible (i.e., your services must be an exact fit with the stated needs) and often require the ability to closely track and report services and expenditures.

- **CORPORATE GIFTS:** Corporate giving makes up only a very small percentage of overall contributions, so unless you're in a particularly unique situation, you should not expect this type of funding to comprise a large portion of your budget. Typically the odds are best when your project is aligned with a company's business objectives. That having been said, corporate funding can be beneficial as it relates to sponsorships of events and activities, securing product for auctions/prizes and small grants that benefit the local community. Many nonprofits also benefit from arranging volunteer opportunities with employees of large companies in their local area and involving key executives as board members. In addition to providing valuable support, it helps to establish relationships with the business sector.

▶ Don't forget to remind donors that their employers may have a matching gift program. Be sure to collect employer information (so you can follow up as necessary) and let them know where to submit the request for the match.

NO. 2

▶ It's important to create a balance between the many sources of contributions. It's also worth noting that in-kind donations and volunteer services — particularly if they're products and services for which you would have otherwise paid — are also types of fundraising.

Don't forget that many companies also have matching gift programs. Remind donors of this during the giving process. Be sure to collect employer information (so you can follow up as necessary) and let them know where to submit any paperwork.

- **PLANNED GIVING:** Planned giving is the transfer of assets (e.g., real estate, stock or life insurance) to a designated nonprofit organization during a lifetime or upon someone's passing. Usually this happens via a will or other written means. The giving is "planned" because often these assets are not liquid, have tax consequences or can be used to simultaneously generate income for donors. Planned gifts are frequently larger than annual campaign or one-time gifts and offer the donor a means of ensuring their philanthropic legacy. Planned gifts often can offer nonprofit organizations sustainability for the future. Planned giving programs are often perceived as complicated, but low-cost strategies such starting a "legacy society" and working with a pro-bono legal or community foundation partner can help simplify the process and reduce costs.

- **ANNUAL CAMPAIGNS:** As the name would imply, these are fixed-time fundraising campaigns that take place annually. They are often board-driven, meaning that the board is actively engaged in soliciting donations and will often jumpstart the campaign with their own commitments (see question 7 of this section for a related discussion of the board's role). Annual campaigns are usually centered on a specific fundraising goal that is made public. If it's practical, the beginning and end can be marked with a special event that recognizes donors, engages corporate sponsors and showcases programs to the media.

- **FEES FOR SERVICE:** Nonprofits of all sizes use fees for mission-related services to meet programmatic and operating needs. These can include membership dues, publication costs or fees for conferences, seminars and trainings. For more information on this type of revenue generation, see Chapter 2: Legal.

❝ You make a living by what you get. You make a life by what you give. ❞

- Winston Churchill

Q How do I know my organization is ready for fundraising?

A Believe it or not, some nonprofit organizations don't have to fundraise. For example, those that are supported entirely by membership dues or act as a social enterprise may not need to raise funds beyond those they already have. However, they are always trying to get people interested in signing up or investing in a cause or mission.

So when is it time to start fundraising? The moment you decide there is a mission or cause that requires the support of many to bring about meaningful change. That said, to ready yourself for fundraising, it's advisable to apply for and gain 501(c)(3) status, along with tax-exempt status in your own state. This will enable individuals' donations to be tax deductible and meet the requirements of philanthropic funders. This is especially important if you anticipate ongoing fundraising targeting multiple sources. However, gaining 501(c)(3) status may not be necessary if you're considering a one-time event such as a conference or film festival.

Fundraising also requires you to have your finances in order. Having accurate and verifiable financial records is a key consideration for many donors. At a minimum, individuals want to understand how much of their donation is going to the program(s) and the difference it will make. In fact, foundations expect it, along with a higher level of reporting, often including audited financial statements.

This chapter helps to outline some of the steps associated with developing a fundraising plan and offers resources to support you in that effort. For more information on the legal and financial considerations associated with fundraising, see Chapters 2 and 4, respectively.

Finally, to advance a truly successful fundraising effort, you'll need to have your brand in order. This is your organization's identity; it's who you are. Effective fundraising requires potential donors to be aware of, understand and feel a connection to your brand. This is important: Any development effort conducted before a brand is established is likely to have unsuccessful results. For more information on branding, see Chapter 6.

If your organization's goals and expenses go beyond the assets you have or expect to bring in, it's time to develop a fundraising plan.

QUICK TIP

No.
4

Q | What are the different types
of funding?

A | There are many different types of funding, but they usually
fall into three main categories:

- **RESTRICTED FUNDS** are to be used only for a specific purpose. This
is the case, for example, when a foundation supports a particular
project or you are awarded a government grant to provide a
specified service in a specified community. Individuals may also
place restrictions on their gift, such as designating it to purchase
library books or computers.

- **UNRESTRICTED FUNDS** are available for use in any way that
furthers the organization's mission (or, to use a fancy tax term, its
exempt purposes). It's often used for operating support, which has
been called the holy grail of fundraising or to cover programmatic
shortfalls. These funds typically arise through individual
donations and fundraising events, but some foundations also
provide such support.

- **BRIDGE FUNDING** (also called temporary funding) is used to
meet a short-term need when there's an expectation that the
organization will be solvent after the fixed time. This can occur,
for example, in the event of a natural disaster, political unrest or
when grants or contract funding are promised but have not yet
been received.

It's wise for nonprofits to have written policies in place regarding how
these types of funding are treated in financial books and separately
accounted for, and when to decline certain types of funding. For
example, expecting a small, restricted donation to support a program
that's not already operational may be unrealistic.

It's worth noting that these are broad categories of support. Other
types of funding — such as endowment support, in-kind contributions,
executive loans, seed money, capital funding, program-related
investments (essentially below-market-rate loans), capital support,
etc. — can also be critical to your nonprofit organization's success.

**Familiarize yourself with the types of funding available and put a policy in place
as to how to account for different types of funding.**

QUICK TIP

Q | Why is it important to diversify fundraising? How do you define the right mix for your organization?

A | If there's one thing the economic downturn has taught us – as individuals or as nonprofit organizations – it's that diversification is key. Philanthropic and corporate funding sway alongside the economy. In a booming economy, they have more money to give (and in the case of foundations, they have more money that they must give).

There's no simple formula that will apply to all nonprofit organizations. For example, an organization that provides job training to low-income people and is customized to meet the needs of specific large employers is likely to cultivate more corporate funding than the average organization. A scientific research institution may rely largely on government funding. Nevertheless, it's a safe bet that you shouldn't be putting all your eggs in one basket. The most important thing is to achieve a balance of funding that's reliable, flexible and diversified enough to meet your needs.

A good starting point is to look at where charitable contributions come from. According to *Giving USA 2011* by the Giving USA Foundation, charitable funding in 2010 (the most recent year available) broke down as follows:

- Individuals: $211.8 billion (73%)
- Foundations: $41 billion (14%)
- Bequests: $22.8 billion (8%)
- Corporations: $15.3 billion (5%)

These are charitable contributions. According to *The Nonprofit Sector in Brief: Public Charities, Giving, and Volunteering, 2010,* by the Urban Institute, government sources account for 32 percent of total nonprofit revenue and more than 24 percent of fees for service (such as through Medicare and Medicaid).

Therefore, your best course of action is to take a close look at your own sources of funding, your organization's unique resources, as well as funding trends in your specific area of focus. It's also important to understand who you're competing with and where their funds are coming from. These insights will give you a good sense of the right funding mix for your organization. From there, you'll want to establish goals and adjust strategies to meet your needs.

▸ Funding diversification is a must for most nonprofits. Take a close look at your sources of funding to see which sectors you might be relying on too heavily, or not enough. Assess the reliability and flexibility of this funding, then adjust your fundraising plan accordingly.

No.
6

Q | What are the basics for developing and implementing a fundraising plan?

A Your plan is a road map that outlines your approach to fundraising via any (or all) of the fundraising sources described in question 2 of this chapter. One of the most important aspects of any plan is the case statement. This should succinctly explain why your issue and organization are great investments for a funder. It might, for example, point to research that demonstrates how effective your type of intervention is from an economic, health and/or social standpoint. It should also serve to differentiate your organization, implicitly conveying why donors should give to your organization above all others. The power of this message, and your ability to constantly communicate it, will underpin all of your fundraising efforts.

The fundraising plan also outlines who you're going to target, for what programs and for how much. Importantly, it aligns with your mission, identifies the strategies and tactics you'll employ to connect with prospects and sets a timeline for implementation. Done properly, the plan can be a critical roadmap to determine where you want to go and how you're going to get there. Your fundraising plan is an important test of whether your overall organizational plan is realistic, as it sets the direction for your staff and also serves as an important tool to engage your board — see question 7 of this chapter for more on that topic.

It's useful to separate your plan into types of donors (e.g., foundations, high-net-worth individuals, the public, etc.), as the strategies for reaching each of these will vary drastically. Once you've identified the types of donors you'll be targeting, identify them specifically. This won't be practical in the case of the general public, but each of the other areas should be populated with specific individuals and organizations you plan to approach. Try to be thorough; but remember, you can always add to these in the future as new opportunities arise.

From there, create a strategy for how you plan to reach your prospective donor. This should be a blend of the funding needed by the organization and the interests and desires of the prospect.

BEFORE YOU DEVELOP YOUR FULL PLAN:

▸ Start with your mission, organization plan and budget, and outline the programs and services for which funding is sought.

▸ Review historical data (past budgets and fundraising efforts) to estimate future needs and identify where you have or have not been successful.

▸ Determine your fundraising goals for each program and for operating costs — these will arise out of your operational budget.

▸ Assess sources of previous funding and establish realistic goals to diversify your funding base if necessary.

For example, if you're developing a new web-based educational platform, your message to an education funder might be quite different than your message to a technology company. The latter might be more interested in the technology component than the content.

For each fundraising activity, outline the tasks required, timeline, lead staff, implementation cost and fundraising goals. This will establish a system to which individuals can be held accountable and give a good picture of the amount of staff or board effort required.

ONE OTHER THING: Most states require you to register if you plan to solicit funds there (and this can get sticky if you're raising money online). The Multi-State Filer Project, organized by the National Association of State Charities Officials and the National Association of Attorneys General, eases that process with the Unified Registration Statement (www.multistatefiling.org) – a single application that's accepted by all but three of the states requiring registration.

▸ It's a simple truth: If you run a nonprofit, you need a fundraising plan.

❝ *In good times and bad, we know that people give because you meet needs, not because you have needs.* ❞

- Kay Sprinkel Grace, Organizational Consultant

Raising money in another state or online? The Multi-State Filer Project makes registering to solicit funds easy. Learn more at www.multistatefiliing.org.

QUICK TIP

N⁰.**7**

Q } What is a nonprofit board's role in fundraising? How can/should they be involved?

A } Board members' specific roles vary from one organization to the next, depending on the nonprofit's needs and structure. Broadly speaking, there is usually an expectation that the board will play some role in fundraising. The trick is ensuring that the nonprofit staff and board have the same expectation.

Your board members should be actively involved in the development of your fundraising plan. They can be some of your best resources in terms of making introductions, and many times they have business expertise that can be useful in developing a sound plan.

The specific role your board will play should be a key part of your fundraising plan. If you don't have one already, develop a board fundraising policy in partnership with the board. This establishes the amount each director is expected to give and raise, the process for waiving the requirement (for example, if your board includes clients), additional expectations (such as captaining a table at an annual dinner) and the ways board members can support fundraising.

▶ For most nonprofits, there is some expectation that board members will be involved in fundraising. The trick is ensuring that the nonprofit staff and board members have the same expectation.

In addition to committing funds, here are a few other ways your board members can be involved:

- Identify new prospects and opportunities for fundraising.

- Identify and cultivate high-net-worth donors.

- Sell tickets to an annual dinner or event.

- Make introductions to potential donors and corporate sponsors.

- Host special meetings or events.

- Accompany the executive director to key meetings with potential donors.

Remember, not all board members are going to be experienced fundraisers. Some even may resist the idea. Work with each member to identify the ways she or he is most comfortable bringing resources to the organization. Consider offering training sessions to increase your directors' capacity and comfort level. The Center for Nonprofit Management (www.cnmsocal.org) and BoardSource (www.boardsource.org) offer a number of trainings to address these issues. Also try role-playing exercises at your next meeting. They can provide a great way to understand (and refine) the messages being delivered and boost confidence.

Q | How can communications help fundraising succeed?

A First, let's define communications. Fundamentally speaking, communications is any activity that enables you to speak outwardly to your stakeholders – e.g., current and potential donors, volunteers, beneficiaries, community leaders, the media, your staff, etc. It allows you to tell a story about your organization, convey why you're necessary, establish how you're different from everything else out there and identify the value you provide to your target audiences.

Communications is fundamental to fundraising. Individuals are often driven by an emotional connection to an issue. Foundations are more likely to fund (and better yet, seek out) an organization they have heard of. Corporations seek projects that enhance their brand, boost the bottom line or raise employee morale (as with a volunteer effort). All of these things can be achieved through communications.

That's why a communications strategy is critical. It identifies where you want to be and serves as a roadmap for how you'll get there. Importantly, it also lays out what you want to communicate to achieve your objectives, and to whom you will communicate it.

Social networking is a perfect example of a communications function that can support fundraising efforts. This is a place where you can engage people who care about your issue and organization. But how are you doing so? Are you providing consistent opportunities to be part of your issue? Are you sharing news articles that keep people apprised of important happenings, whether or not you're mentioned? Are you acknowledging donors – large and small? Are you responding to people who have tweeted positive messages? Are you telling the story of your organization and beneficiaries? If you aren't, you should be. These are examples of activities that not only help to build awareness of your organization, but create an ongoing connection with past, current and potential donors.

RELATIONSHIPS ARE EVERYTHING – whether they're developed electronically, in print or in-person – and strategic communications can help you develop them. That's why we've devoted a whole chapter to the topic. Check out Chapter 6 for more on how communications can advance your objectives.

▶ Communications allows you to position your organization to a variety of stakeholders in a way that enables them to understand why your mission is important, why it's needed in the areas you serve and why your organization is the best one to carry out the work. When target audiences understand these things, you'll find the path to raising funds is a whole lot easier.

NO.
9

Q } What are the fundamentals of successful grantwriting?

A } First and foremost, follow the rules. It doesn't matter how dedicated you are to your mission or how important you believe it is (and, yes, it probably is), every foundation has funding guidelines and straying from them is a waste of everyone's time. If a funder donates exclusively in Louisiana, don't apply if your organization is based in California. If they request a two-page letter of intent, don't send three. And, make sure to send all requested attachments. Anything else will quickly result in a trip to the recycling bin.

Here are the things you need to prepare for a successful grant application:

- Set your funding goals, research and identify appropriate funders, and learn as much as possible about the prospective foundations.

- Be strategic about what you will request from each funder. Identify how much money you need and your plan for raising it, and lay out how much has already been committed (note: it's a lot easier for a funder to commit $100,000 to a $10 million project that's 80 percent funded than 0 percent funded).

- Clearly define the program or activity for which you are requesting funding.

- Define your program's connection to the foundation's goals and values.

- Define the need for your project among the community being served; describe the potential impact specifically.

- Develop a program budget that spells out income and expenses.

- Be clear about what success will look like and how you'll know it has been achieved.

WRITING A GRANT REQUEST?

▸ Be clear about who you are, the details of the program for which you're seeking funding, the expected impact and other sources of support. And always, always follow the rules.

Funders are very specific about what they want. So, be sure to follow funding guidelines or your application will not be accepted.

QUICK TIP

- Identify potential references for funders that may require them.

- Prepare the most typical proposal attachments, including your organization's financial statements, a board list with affiliation, and beneficiary testimonials, articles, awards or recognition.

With these in place, you'll be in a good position to develop turn-key information for grant applications and make a strong case for why your organization is a good investment. From there, it's a matter of deciding where you'll apply and customizing the application to meet a specific funder's requirements.

You should also know that a number of grantmaker associations have developed common grant applications that enable grant-seekers to submit one application to multiple organizations. The Foundation Center (www.foundationcenter.org) provides a list of associations that accept a common application.

If I can't understand the title, then I don't fund it.

- Whitney Tilt, Grant Reviewer, National Fish & Wildlife Foundation

Visit www.nonprofitanswerguide.org **for timely sector resources and more expert answers to your most immediate nonprofit questions.**

QUICK TIP

N⁰. **10**

Q ⟩ What is e-Philanthropy and online giving?

A ⟩ Online giving is simply the act of donating online. This can be done on your own website, through a third party or by mobile phone. Online giving is the central component of e-philanthropy, which uses technology (mainly the Internet) to connect people with opportunities to donate money or find volunteer opportunities. Another important aspect of e-philanthropy is using technology to maintain relationships with donors, supporters and volunteers. Many organizations are successfully interacting with their stakeholders through social media.

e-Philanthropy can be an extremely cost-effective way to fundraise and connect with your audience. There are several services designed to help nonprofits get started. For example, Network for Good (www.networkforgood.org) is a subscription-based service that processes donations, provides an e-newsletter service and enables people to give directly to your organization. GlobalGiving (www.globalgiving.org) is another forum that enables people to contribute to more than 800 projects featured on its website for a 15 percent fulfillment fee. Facebook also offers a resource site for nonprofits, including success stories, applications, plug-ins and suggestions for maximizing your presence on the site.

As for mobile campaigns, these are easier now than ever. You've probably seen ads to text "give" to a short phone number (called an SMS short code) to automatically have a $5 or $10 donation added to your cell phone bill. These have been particularly prevalent during natural disasters, but many nonprofits are integrating mobile giving into their regular fundraising efforts.

Wondering how to get started with your mobile campaign? Fortunately there are a few organizations that have already put the technology in place and made the necessary deals with wireless carriers. Check out the mGive Foundation (www.mgivefoundation.org) or the Mobile Giving Foundation (www.mobilegiving.org) to see if this might be part of your fundraising mix.

BLOGS

- **Nonprofit Tech 2.0: A Social Media Guide for Nonprofits**
  (www.nonprofitorgs.wordpress.com)

GRANT RESOURCES

- **FindRFP**
  (www.findrfp.com)

- **Foundation Directory Online**
  (www.fconline.foundationcenter.org)

- **Grants.gov**

- **Philanthropy News Digest**
  (www.foundationcenter.org/pnd)

- **USA.gov**

- **GrantStation**

- **DonorsChoose**

FUNDRAISING CONSULTANTS

- **Center for Nonprofit Management**
  (www.cnmsocal.org)

LEADERSHIP RESOURCES

- **Association of Fundraising Professionals**
  (www.afpnet.org)

- **BoardSource**
  (www.boardsource.org)

- **Foundation Center**
  (www.foundationcenter.org)

- **Independent Sector**
  (www.independentsector.org)

E-PHILANTHROPY RESOURCES

- **GlobalGiving**
  (www.globalgiving.org)

- **mGive Foundation**
  (www.mgivefoundation.org)

- **Mobile Giving Foundation**
  (www.mobilegiving.org)

- **Network for Good**
  (www.networkforgood.org)

READY-TO-GO-RESOURCES

20-SECOND-SUMMARY

- Fundraising starts with your organization's mission and is an important way to involve others in supporting the cause.

- Create realistic expectations. Analyze previous fundraising efforts and the success of organizations similar to yours.

- Fundraising is an ongoing process. Be open to refining your plan as circumstances, lessons learned and new opportunities warrant it.

- Boards can and should be an asset to fundraising. The more you engage leadership, the more successful you'll be. Set expectations in partnership with your board and assess whether there's a need for training.

- Relationships are essential. Invest the time to establish strong relationships — with individuals, corporations and foundations — and the funding will follow.

- Most states require you to register if you plan to fundraise there. The Unified Registration Statement makes the process easier. It's accepted in all but three of the states that require you to register.

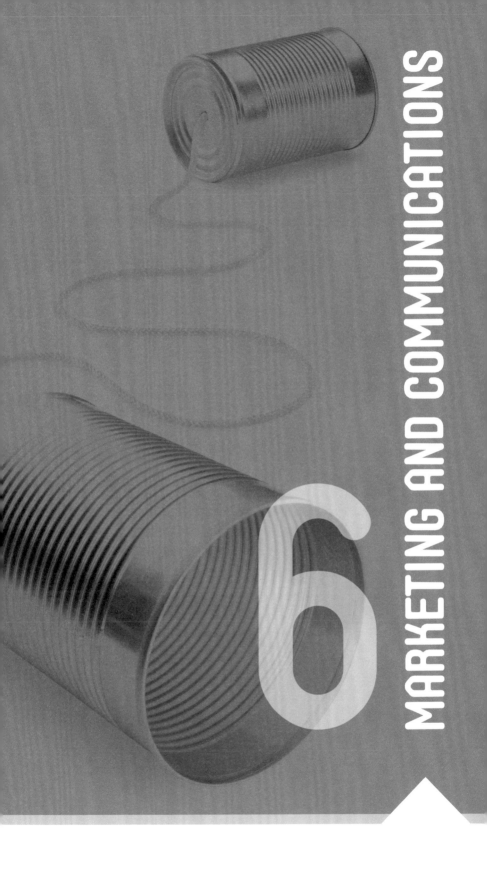

MARKETING AND COMMUNICATIONS

You need to spread the word about your organization to raise money, but you don't have any money to spread the word.

So you're left only to imagine what life would be like if everyone knew about your organization, the work it does, and why it's so important. We've all been there.

For a lot of nonprofits, marketing and communications take a backseat to program activities. We get it. You're driven by your mission, not by marketing. But effectively communicating about your organization **will** advance your mission. It's how you get people behind your cause, raise awareness, engage volunteers, stimulate giving, access donors and connect with your beneficiaries.

There are a lot of great reasons to hire a consultant for marketing and communications (and we explain the "why" and "how" of it here), but you may not be financially ready for that yet. That's why we've outlined the basic steps that go into strategic communications planning in this chapter. We also share guidance on establishing a brand identity, developing key messages, positioning your organization for success and the importance of storytelling.

It's going to take some time and commitment, but the dividends can far outweigh the initial investment.

Q | What are the first steps in developing a strategic communications plan?

A | You want to raise awareness and funds for your cause. To do that, you need to get your message out, to engage and motivate your audiences. But how do you cut through the information clutter to ensure your voice is heard above the rest? In today's competitive market, your approach to communications is key.

Thinking strategically about communications will help you tailor your activities to meet your constituent needs. It'll help you budget for the tools and strategies you'll need to use. And, it'll help you link communications to your goals and mission, to ensure you're getting the right results.

RESEARCH TO GET A TRUE PICTURE AND ESTABLISH A BASELINE FOR MEASURING SUCCESS.

Research is critical to getting a clear picture of who you are as an organization and where you want to go. It'll also help you learn who your audiences are and more clearly see the landscape in which you operate. Getting this kind of insight is necessary to develop a plan based on fact rather than assumptions.

To start, you'll want to conduct an audit of your organization. Take an objective look at your mission and goals, and your current communications activities. Who are you? How are you perceived in the market? Who are your donors and why do they give? Is your mission clear? Are your goals in line with your mission?

Outline the communications activities you've implemented and the results you've achieved. Ask staff for input. Tap constituents, board members and other keys stakeholders for an outsider's perspective.

Once you know who you are and how you're perceived, you'll want to look at your organization in relation to your peers. What are peer organizations doing well? What challenges do they face? Whom do they serve? And what makes them unique?

Knowing how you compare to others that serve your mission will allow you to unlock your specific strengths and communicate the unique

▶ Without exception, effective communications strategies are built on a solid foundation of research and planning.

A good communications plan uses background research to outline objectives, strategies and tactics that will get you where you want to go. And, don't forget to include a budget, timeline and metrics.

QUICK TIP

No. 1

**EIGHT QUESTIONS
TO ASK BEFORE
DEVELOPING YOUR
PLAN.**

▶ Do you know your
   mission and goals?

▶ Are your
   communications
   strategies oriented
   toward your goals?

▶ What communications
   challenges are you
   facing today?

▶ What marketing and
   communications
   strategies are popular
   in your service area?

▶ Who are your audiences
   (constituent groups,
   partners, funders)?

▶ What do your target
   audiences know
   about you?

▶ What is your staff
   skill-set?

▶ Does your budget
   adequately support
   your communications
   activities and can you
   afford to hire additional
   resources if needed?

value your organization contributes. This will help you drive a clear,
focused mission that will resonate with your constituents and allow
you to stay relevant to them.

FOUR TOOLS YOU CAN USE TO MAKE RESEARCH EASY AND COST-EFFECTIVE.

1. **SURVEYS.** Use web survey tools like SurveyMonkey™ and Constant
Contact® to develop and disseminate questionnaires to staff and
constituents about specific issues. Use phone surveys to elicit even
more revealing results.

2. **FOCUS GROUPS.** Conduct short sessions with donors, volunteers,
colleagues, board members and other key stakeholders to test the
effectiveness of your communications materials and get in-depth
information about how others perceive you.

3. **COMMUNICATIONS AUDITS.** Generally conducted by a consultant, an
audit is typically an in-depth analysis of your current communications
strategies. It provides feedback to help you identify gaps and learn
which activities are working and which aren't.

4. **SECONDARY INFORMATION SOURCES.** Already existing nonprofit-
related research, such as statistical reports, news items, trend
reports and the like, is readily available (often online) and usually
free. This kind of sector-specific information can help you better
understand the nonprofit landscape and your competitors.

CREATE A ROADMAP TO GUIDE YOU TO YOUR GOAL.

Once you know who you are and where you want to go, you're going to
need to develop a plan of action. When writing your communications
plan you'll want to:

OUTLINE YOUR OBJECTIVES AND GOALS. Think general and specific,
short and long term. Link goals to your mission to keep you on track.
Make objectives measurable and achievable.

IDENTIFY YOUR AUDIENCES. You may have more than one. (Consider
constituent groups, potential partners and funders.) If so, segment
and prioritize them.

**HIGHLIGHT YOUR UNIQUE POSITION AMONG YOUR PEERS AND TIE THIS
TO YOUR CONSTITUENT NEEDS.** What makes you stand out and why is
this important to your audience?

IDENTIFY KEY MESSAGES THAT RESONATE WITH EACH AUDIENCE. Think
of the most important things you want your audience to know about
your organization and what it does to help them.

DESCRIBE THE STRATEGIES AND TOOLS YOU'LL USE TO REACH YOUR GOAL. Will you focus on creating partnerships to get your messages out? Will you use social media or direct mail? Donor cultivation and fundraising? If you're unsure of your options, do an Internet search for nonprofit marketing or communications strategies for ideas.

OUTLINE YOUR BUDGET. You'll want to look at the output you have available for communications activities, upgrading staff skills or hiring additional resources. If you're low on dollars, you'll also want to describe how you'll find the funds to implement your plan.

DESCRIBE YOUR IMPLEMENTATION PLAN. What's your timetable? How will you prioritize the launch of each strategy?

DEVELOP A STRATEGY TO MEASURE SUCCESS. Identify what success will look like and evaluate your progress as you go. Determine what's working and what isn't. Then, you can modify and refine your strategies to make the most of your resources and budget.

Developing a comprehensive plan is not a quick or easy task, but it is essential to advancing your mission. Taking care to ensure organization-wide buy-in and participation will smooth the process and set the stage for development of a great plan.

Half the money I spend on advertising is wasted, I just don't know which half.

- John Wanamaker, Marketing & Advertising Pioneer

Surveys, focus groups, communications audits and secondary information sources are easy, cost-effective tools you can use to help build a communications plan.

QUICK TIP

NO. **2**

Q Why do I need a strong brand or organizational identity? How do we establish the values and attributes that describe our brand? And what's a brand anyway?

BENEFITS OF BUILDING A BRAND:

▸ Provides a foundation for developing an appropriate graphic identity.

▸ Provides a framework to communicate mission, programs and services.

▸ Results in constituent loyalty, increased public support and, in turn, increased revenue.

A Think of your brand or organizational identity like your individual identity. It's who you are in your entirety. It's your organization's DNA.

In the corporate world, brands rule. But program-focused nonprofits often overlook the value of creating a brand or organizational identity, not fully recognizing the power brands have. A strong brand not only helps to position an organization at a desired level in their service area, but it can also move constituents to action. It helps develop trust and, in turn, loyalty, allowing organizations to create sustainable relationships with their constituents.

A brand is what makes you unique. It's the most important tool you have, to build confidence in your organization from within. Branding helps you clarify what you stand for and, in turn, helps you communicate your position to your audience in a way that resonates.

HOW DO YOU DEVELOP YOURS?

A BRAND IS OFTEN COMMUNICATED THROUGH THREE ELEMENTS:

1. a brand purpose,

2. a brand personality and

3. a brand promise.

THINK ABOUT YOUR ORGANIZATION'S PURPOSE. Start by defining what you do and what makes you unique. Develop a purpose statement (like a mission statement) explaining why you exist strategically and what you do. By defining your purpose, you're developing a foundation on which you can build focused goals and consistent communication.

Visit www.nonprofitanswerguide.org for timely sector resources and more expert answers to your most immediate nonprofit questions.

QUICK TIP

DESCRIBE YOUR BRAND PERSONALITY. Your brand personality is an expression of your core values and the relationship you have with your constituents; it's described using human traits. Are you innovative or traditional? Friendly? Approachable? Responsive? These traits will give life to your organization on the inside, guide your approach to communications and help you define your graphic identity.

DEVELOP A BRAND PROMISE. A brand promise is about benefits. It's the emotional part of your brand purpose. It's what gives your employees, colleagues, board members, constituents and other stakeholders confidence in your organization. Tap into your strengths and develop an informed promise based on constituent and competitor research.

GET BUY-IN. Once you've developed your brand, you need to get everyone in your organization to support and steward it. This includes management, staff, consultants and your board.

Remember, your organization already has a brand. The key to success is to manage it. Manage your brand right and you'll carve a niche in your market, create a clear-sighted organization, build consistent communications and instill confidence and trust at every touchpoint.

No. 2

A BRAND IS MORE THAN A LOGO AND A TAGLINE!

▶ Your logo and tagline reinforce your brand, but they are not your brand. Your brand is the sum of all you do. It's reflected in your corporate culture, the way you communicate, the relationships you build and the promises you make to your audience.

❝ *A brand for a company is like a reputation for a person. You earn reputation by trying to do hard things well.* ❞

- Jeff Bezos, CEO, Amazon

Branding a nonprofit isn't any different than branding a corporation, product or well-known person. It's about building trust and conveying your organization's unique attributes.

QUICK TIP

NO.**3**

Q | What is messaging? How are key messages developed?

A Simply put, messaging is a term to describe how you talk about who you are and why you exist as an organization. It communicates key points you consistently make when you reach out to your audience. And it always ties back to your brand.

Different messages can be developed for different purposes, such as speeches, fundraising campaigns or presentations. They should also be developed for different audiences. You may want to consider crafting a set of short, standard phrases or paragraphs to describe your organization, programs and services. Then, as you need to reach out to specific audiences, implement new campaigns or communicate programs, you'll have standard language ready to tailor to your purpose.

A well-crafted message will highlight your unique benefits, target your audience, support your mission and often include a call to action. Follow these three steps to develop messages that motivate.

1. Think about what you want people to know about your organization and your cause. What do you want them to say about you? What do you want them to do?

2. Develop a few core messages that connect the dots between what you do and how it relates to your audience. Develop messages around a single idea. Keep language simple and use analogies or personal stories to get your point across. Make your messages believable. Provide evidence such as numbers to increase credibility.

3. Be consistent with delivery. Each message you deliver should reflect your brand — that is, who you are. Highlight what is relevant to the issue and your audience, but be sure to include a consistent statement about your organization. This makes your messaging memorable and helps position you in the market and in the minds of your audience.

Slogans or taglines illustrate the art of focusing your message. Here are three great slogans for inspiration:

▶ "A mind is a terrible thing to waste." United Negro College Fund

▶ "Live strong." Lance Armstrong Foundation

▶ "Take a bite out of crime." National Crime Prevention Council

Source: *Cause Communications Toolkit*

Once you've developed your messages, test them out! Use your messages with key target audiences to understand what's working, or not. Refine as necessary.

QUICK TIP

Q What's an elevator speech and why should I have one?

A One of the most important things nonprofit leaders can do, especially when they're the spokespeople for their organization, is to develop an elevator speech. Being able to sum up your programs and services and communicate them clearly and quickly, are the most effective ways to reach out at any encounter.

An elevator speech is simply a short description of what you do and why it's important. You should be able to deliver it in the time it takes to take an elevator ride (typically 30 seconds or less).

An elevator speech should say a lot in a few words. And it should grab a listener's attention and make him or her want to know more.

Let's say you run a health clinic that serves children from low-income families. Your elevator speech for a funder interested in child health or community development might look something like this:

The Impact Clinic provides critical health services to low-income children under age 2. In 10 years, our volunteer doctors and nurses have delivered check-ups, immunizations, screenings for health issues and medication to over 30,000 children. We work on a sliding scale that covers 70 percent of our costs. We're the only clinic within 10 miles and we serve more than half of the area's low-income families.

Parents tell us if Impact Clinic didn't exist, their children wouldn't receive the care they need. That's exactly the problem the Metro neighborhood has. Impact is the nearest clinic and it takes two hours to reach us by bus. Children there are 25 percent less likely to receive immunizations as kids in our area. That's why we're partnering with Metro Community Foundation to build a new clinic in Metro. I'd love to talk with you more about our approach and alignment with your funding interests. May I have your card to schedule a meeting?

In this example, we've highlighted why our fictitious organization is essential to the local community, quickly conveyed what the organization does and for whom, pulled out key stats and used the data as a lead-in to an expansion project.

Note that we've included a call to action at the end. This puts the speaker in control of next steps, which is important given that your ultimate goal should be to get an opportunity to share more detail.

An elevator speech helps to reinforce your brand. It allows everyone — staff, management and the board — to speak with one voice and tell a concise, compelling story.

WHEN DEVELOPING YOUR ELEVATOR SPEECH:

▸ Think about your market and the problems you're trying to help solve.

▸ Think about solutions. What does success look like?

▸ Highlight your organization's unique differences. What makes you stand out in the market?

▸ Consider using stories. Can you incorporate a personal experience that illustrates your impact in the community?

NO. **5**

Q How can we use storytelling to effectively position our organization?

A People remember stories. They engage, inspire and encourage people to act. For nonprofits, they can be used effectively in just about any method of communication.

All nonprofits have stories to tell about how their constituency was impacted through their work. But many organizations don't fully recognize the power their stories have to help them connect with their audience. Storytelling is one of the most important devices in your communications toolkit. How better to illustrate your impact than to "show" your constituents a successful outcome?

HOW STORYTELLING CAN BENEFIT YOUR MESSAGING:

- Stories "show" your reader rather than "telling" them. They help position you as an expert and build trust among your audience.

- Stories are memorable and touch readers in a personal way.

- Stories help you focus your message to avoid communicating too much unnecessary information.

- Stories help you bring independent pieces of information together into a coherent message.

Think about using storytelling in annual reports, on your website, in newsletters, fundraising campaigns and direct mail. Keep stories short and relevant to your audience, and make them about a single person or group of people. And don't forget to deliver an underlying message that ties back to your mission and goals.

▸ "Storyless" narratives rely on dry data and program descriptions without ever bringing the content to life. The result is a lost audience. Instead … tell a great story!

▸ The best stories have a beginning, a middle and an end. Establish heroes and villains. Create conflict and use an emotional hook.

Source: *Cause Communications Toolkit*

Q How do we create a budget for communications?

A Budgeting for communications starts with your communications plan, as discussed in question 1 of this chapter. Once you've outlined the communications strategies and tactics you'll undertake to achieve your objectives, the path toward developing a budget should be quite a bit clearer. Just as with your organizational budget, you'll want to plan for and track expenses by category (e.g., advertising, salaries, design, special events, to name a few).

When you write your communications plan, you should be allotting a dollar cost to each strategy you include. Make sure you do your research. Be realistic about resources and timelines needed to create, implement, monitor and evaluate each strategy. A delayed project, for example, can eat up resources, significantly affecting costs.

When you transfer these costs to your communications budget, you'll want to list out each project and detail all associated costs. You also may want to consider adding a line item for contingencies. If you allow for unexpected expenses in advance, you won't be forced to abandon a strategy if its associated costs are more than you anticipated.

Another important factor is to distinguish between your organizational communications budget and those of specific programs. Of course, this is worthwhile in terms of understanding and managing your overall budget. However, it's also important because integrating communications into overall program planning (and related grant requests) demonstrates a sophisticated, holistic approach to realizing your mission.

Funders understand the return on investment associated with communications activity that supports mission-related goals. By ensuring communications is a core function across your organization, you will position your organization as a far more attractive and strategic investment in the eyes of funders. Indeed, support for communications should be built into your grant requests as a matter of course. Doing so will set the stage for you to deliver on your own goals, as well as those of your funder.

- Track expenses as they happen and measure ROI to help you sell your budgetary needs.

- Detail expenditures as you go and analyze costs versus benefits. This will help you tailor future communications for greater return on investment. It will also help you communicate what's working to your board and funders, to grow your budget down the road.

- And be sure to build an extra month or two into timelines to account for any refinements to strategy and implementation that arise out of your results.

Need budgeting help? Pick up a copy of Budgeting for Not-for-Profit Organizations, **by David Maddox.**

QUICK TIP

NO. **7**

Q | Why is it important for fundraising and marketing communications to align?

A | How can you raise money for your cause if no one knows about the good work you're doing?

HOW MARKETING COMMUNICATIONS SUPPORTS YOUR FUNDRAISING ACTIVITIES:

▸ Strong communications help you build awareness for your organization and cause. This foundation builds a pipeline for fundraising activities and facilitates the "ask."

▸ Clear, consistent and targeted messaging gives your staff and board the tools they need to create fundraising programs that get results.

▸ A strong brand identity helps your organization speak with a single voice, delivering a clear message that resonates with current and future donors.

▸ A clear call to action ensures that your target audiences know what to do after being motivated by your message.

Successful fundraising is founded on making a strong case for your cause. In fact, recent data shows that when an organization's communications strategies are clear and focused, its fundraising dollars increase substantially.

When communications and fundraising are in sync, one supports the other through simple, consistent, compelling messages, delivered in a way that builds trust. Trust makes people want to get involved, support your cause and donate dollars.

Effective communications for fundraising is transparent, delivers on your brand promise and always reflects your organizational identity. This ensures messaging is believable and memorable, helping you to build trust among new donors and loyalty among donors you already have.

HOW TO SUPPORT FUNDRAISING WITH COMMUNICATIONS.

TIE COMMUNICATIONS TO FUNDRAISING INITIATIVES. Ensure messages are in sync with fundraising goals. Determine what you want to achieve and when. Use tools and vehicles that target the audience, clearly communicate what you want people to do, and always tie back to your brand.

USE STORIES TO SUPPORT YOUR EFFORTS. Stories make your cause personal. They touch donor emotions and "show" your audience the difference you're making. They can also be used over a period of time to draw an audience in and keep them coming back for more.

RELEASE GOOD NEWS AS SOON AS IT HAPPENS. Keep your audience informed and excited about your cause. All staff should be looking for good news stories. Try using press releases and case studies on your website and in email communications to get the word out about the work you're doing before the information gets old. Need help? The Center for Civic Partnerships has compiled a variety of free resources to help nonprofits develop their media and public relations efforts (www.civicpartnerships.org, click on "tools and resources").

Q } What role does the board play in communications? How can board members be effectively engaged?

A } An organization's communications are only as strong as the people who deliver them – this includes a nonprofit board. Your board is key to your communications and fundraising activities, as it embodies your brand and tells your story to raise dollars, create strategic partnerships and cultivate resources.

Ideally, you'll have board buy-in to your brand purpose, personality and promise. And your board will fully understand the relationship between clear, consistent and compelling communications and the ability to move your mission forward. Developing a comprehensive strategic communications plan that illustrates how communications will help the organization achieve objectives will help in this regard.

Once you have board buy-in, you'll want to engage the members to support your efforts. Here are some ideas to grow board involvement:

POSITION YOUR BOARD AS AMBASSADORS FOR YOUR CAUSE. As stewards, your board should be able to convey key messages and drive your brand forward at the community level. Provide board members with the tools they need to do so by keeping them informed of the good work you're doing. You may also want to consider bringing in a consultant to provide communications training and help board members become comfortable in this role. If funds are a challenge, seek out pro brono services through organizations such as Taproot Foundation (www.taprootfoundation.org). You'll also want to research local organizations that provide grants for nonprofit capacity building. State associations for nonprofits and regional associations of grantmakers can serve as useful resources for such research.

As ambassadors, your board members are also ideally positioned to watch trends in the community and report this intelligence back to staff.

SPEAK YOUR BOARD'S LANGUAGE.

▸ Avoid communications jargon when talking to your board. Keep discussion focused on benefits – that is, how communications can help move your mission forward.

Board members can be powerful spokespeople with the media, potential strategic partners, donors and even internal audiences who will benefit from seeing people as excited about the mission as you are.

QUICK TIP

No. 8

FORM A BOARD COMMUNICATIONS COMMITTEE. Developing a formal committee can be an easy way to encourage board involvement on a regular or on an ad hoc basis. A committee can review communications materials and identify gaps, or even provide suggestions for capitalizing on resources and trends in the market. Ideally, you'll have a board member with expertise in the area that can serve as lead. If you don't have an existing board member with expertise in this area, make a priority of recruiting one. Be sure to use the opportunity to reach out to colleagues and partners in the communications industry to grow board participation.

▸ A board-level communications committee can be especially helpful in setting priorities, engaging their fellow board members and potentially leveraging their own expertise from other sectors.

ASK A BOARD MEMBER TO LEAD A HIGH-PROFILE PROJECT. When staff resources are stretched, and key projects could have significant community impact, an expert, connected board member may be an ideal project lead.

USE BOARD CONNECTIONS. Ask board members to reach out to their networks to connect you with communications professionals who can help you meet your goals and objectives. Be sure to keep detailed records of all new connections to help you build relationships over the long term.

❝ Any committee is only as good as the most knowledgeable, determined and vigorous person on it. There must be somebody who provides the flame. ❞

- Lady Bird Johnson

Q | What is social media?
Am I ready to use it?

A As opposed to broadcast media (TV, newspapers, print, etc.), which pushes information out to an audience, social media relies on audience participation as a driver, allowing individuals with common interests to quickly and easily use technology to interact and exchange information in the electronic world.

Social media should be part of your strategic communications plan, simply because it's a fast, cost-effective way to monitor and build your brand and grow relationships with your audience. The key is being ready to use it. It's possible to do more harm than good to your brand and communications objectives if you leap into conversations too soon. Here's how you can get ready to join in:

KNOW WHO YOU ARE AND HOW YOU WANT TO POSITION YOURSELF ONLINE. A strong organizational identity will help you do this. Appoint one or two social media ambassadors to keep communications consistent. Be sure they understand the approach you're aiming for and what's off-limits for online discussion.

BE REALISTIC ABOUT YOUR ABILITY TO MANAGE YOUR SOCIAL MEDIA STRATEGIES. Start slow. Small steps will help you assess the resources you'll need to dedicate to social media to benefit from it.

BEFORE YOU START TALKING ONLINE, LISTEN CAREFULLY. Get a sense of who your audience is and what they're talking about before you chime in. This will ensure you offer relevant information that positions you as an expert.

ENGAGE PEOPLE IN MEANINGFUL INTERACTIONS. It's easy to simply talk at people, but effective social media strategies are about building relationships with your target audience.

Consider posting questions that invite feedback and opinions about issues that matter to your organization. When users post comments that are relevant to your organization, acknowledge them. Use social media as one of the ways you thank individual donors. Most of all, be creative. There are many ways you can build affinity with your audience. Embrace them.

ONCE YOU JOIN THE CONVERSATION, PROTECT YOUR BRAND. Be proactive rather than reactive. Follow conversations about your organization, programs and services. Don't wait to respond if discussion turns negative. The intimate nature of social media encourages open dialogue, and sincere exchange is welcomed.

To learn more about social media, read Chapter 10: Technology and Facilities.

SOCIAL MEDIA IS NOT
ONE-SIZE-FITS-ALL!

▸ Not all social media tools are right for every organization. Know what you can manage and where your audience is talking online. Choose carefully, and use tools that best reach your constituents.

NO. **10**

Q Should I hire an employee or consultant to develop and implement our communications plan?

A In an ideal world, you'd have a department dedicated to communications, staffed by experts in the area. But in the nonprofit sector, employees often wear many hats, simply taking on responsibilities as tasks arise. So, whether you're able to hire an employee or consultant who specializes in communications, will probably come down to what you can afford.

To make the best use of the resources and budget you have, first look at your needs and then assess your staff skill set. Determine the ability of your current employees to develop and tackle the communications strategies you need to meet your goals. Can your in-house resources be diverted to communications work without sacrificing other programs? Do you have a staff member with skills and interest in the area? If so, consider training current staff and prioritizing strategies to what you can manage with the resources you already have.

If you don't have the right skills in-house or you can't sacrifice staff time, you'll want to consider hiring an employee or consultant for the job. Hiring an employee is, of course, a long-term commitment, so to start, you may want to bring in an expert on a project basis. It may be tempting to engage an intern for communications functions, particularly in social media, given how adept young people can be in that space. However, it's important to remember that communications is what drives your organization's external presence so those responsible for it must possess the right skill set.

Project hires can be a cost-effective way to develop a strategic communications plan or implement a single campaign. Sometimes, an outsider's objective point of view, especially during research phase, can also bring a fresh perspective to a project.

If you do choose to hire a consultant for a specific project, you're going to want to find the right fit. Look at track records and creative processes, and always check references. To avoid confusion and maximize time and budget, ensure the scope of the project is clearly defined, with a beginning, a middle and an end. And along the way, be prepared to provide the consultant with the support he or she requires to get the work done effectively.

To learn more hiring consultants, read Chapter 9: Managing People.

SIX GOOD REASONS TO HIRE A CONSULTANT:

▸ No one in-house has the expertise you need.

▸ You have the know-how but not the time.

▸ You're too close to the issue and can't be impartial.

▸ The project is confidential and inappropriate to assign internally.

▸ You need an expert's credentials to help you sell your board.

▸ You need help on several levels, so it's not cost effective to hire a single person.

Source: *Cause Communications Toolkit*

GENERAL

- **Communications Toolkit,** Cause Communications

- **The Next Evolution of Marketing: Connect with Your Customers by Marketing with Meaning,** by Bob Gilbreath

- **The Nonprofit Marketing Guide: High-Impact, Low-Cost Ways to Build Support for Your Good Cause,** (The Jossey-Bass Nonprofit Guidebook Series) by Kivi Leroux Miller

GUERRILLA MARKETING

- **Guerrilla Marketing for Nonprofits,** by Jay Conrad Levinson, Frank Adkins and Chris Forbes

MESSAGING AND STORYTELLING

- **Bang! Getting your Message Heard in a Noisy World,** by Linda Kaplan Thaler and Robin Koval with Delia Marshall

- **Storytelling in Organizations: Why Storytelling is Transforming 21st Century Organizations and Management,** by John Seely Brown, Stephen Denning, Katalina Groh and Laurence Prusak

BLOGS

- **Katya's Non-Profit Marketing Blog** (www.nonprofitmarketingblog.com)

- **Kivi's Nonprofit Communications Blog** (www.nonprofitmarketingguide.com/blog)

- **Seth's Blog** (www.sethgodin.com)

READY-TO-GO-RESOURCES

20-SECOND-SUMMARY

- Manage your brand. Develop a strong organizational identity and let it drive your communications.

- Tell stories to engage and inspire your constituents to act. Keep stories short and relevant to your audience and ensure they deliver an underlying message that ties to your mission.

- Don't jump into social media before you're ready. Ensure those who speak for your organization online understand how to manage and protect your brand.

- Detail communications expenditures as you go. Weigh costs versus benefits to help you see what's working, and better target your communications budget.

- Get your board working for your organization. Form a communications committee and use board members for reviews, feedback and intelligence.

- Look to consultants to take on discreet projects. Contract hires offer specialized expertise, bring an outside perspective and can save you money.

STRATEGIC PLANNING

Some folks will probably cringe when you raise the idea of strategic planning.

They might say, "What's the point when we already know what we're doing?" "We're already overworked, we don't have time for that," or, "That sounds great, but how do we do it?" Then there's the ever popular, "But we already have a strategic plan. It's on that shelf over there."

Give us a few minutes and we'll address those points and more.

This chapter looks at a few approaches to strategic planning. There are many options (and no, they don't all take tons of time and paper), so you'll ultimately need to determine what's best for your organization. Still, there are many components that are common across strategic planning models — mission and vision identification, organization assessments, environmental scans, goal and objective development and metrics, for example. We take a look at all of these here and serve up some user-friendly resources to help you drive things forward.

At the end of the day, your plan should rally everyone around where you want to be and how you're going to get there. Do that, and you'll be a whole lot closer to achieving your mission. And, funders will take you more seriously too.

Q } What is the best way to do planning?

A } There is no single right way to do strategic planning. The best way to do it is the way that suits or will best serve your organization. That's going to depend on your resources, internal capacity, engagement of your staff and board and the goals of your organization.

That said, it's important to approach strategic planning as a collaborative process. Your board and high-level staff should be actively engaged in the development of your plan.

This generates buy-in, ensures diversity of thought and involves them in fundamental choices about the direction of the organization.

The scale and scope of ways to involve your board and staff vary drastically — from completing interviews and questionnaires, to retreats facilitated by an outside consultant, and board committees dedicated to driving the process. What works for you will depend on your organizational culture and resources. As you begin to define your process, we recommend sharing it with key team members for feedback. This will allow you to gauge how realistic it is as it relates to available time, and begin to set expectations with those who will be involved.

Carter McNamara, MBA, Ph.D., author of the *Field Guide to Nonprofit Strategic Planning and Facilitation*, has developed a useful summary of the basic steps of a strategic planning process, which includes:

- Identifying your mission.
- Clarifying the goals that must be achieved to realize your mission.
- Identifying the strategies necessary to achieve each goal.
- Creating action plans needed to implement each goal.
- Monitoring and updating your plan.

▶ Your approach to planning will depend largely on your resources, internal capacity, engagement of your staff and board and the goals of your organization.

Strategic planning is a collaborative process. To ensure success, get your board and high-level staff actively engaged in the development of your plan.

QUICK TIP

No. 1

McNamara also suggests that many organizations evolve from these basics to conduct strategic planning that's based on issues an organization faces, or its specific goals. Such an approach would require an assessment of strengths, weaknesses, opportunities and threats (better known as a SWOT analysis, explained in question 4), an effort that's recommended by many strategic planning professionals.

In recent years, some strategic planners have proposed alternatives to the widely used approach described above. They argue that the traditional strategic planning process takes too much time and is no longer responsive to our rapidly changing world.

For example, in the book *The Nonprofit Strategy Revolution*, by David La Piana proposes that strategy development is a constantly evolving process that neither requires, nor benefits from, an isolated strategic planning process. The author proposes a model that, among other things, identifies criteria that are evaluated in real time to determine whether a particular strategy will be implemented.

The point is, there's no right or wrong way to plan. The most important thing is to take a look at the available options and figure out what approach offers the best match with your organizational culture and resources.

▶ Take time to research different approaches to planning. A quick Internet search for "nonprofit strategic planning books" will yield a lot of helpful results. Take a look at the reviews and you're likely to find a few that are well-suited to your organization's culture.

" A goal without a plan, is just a wish. "

- John Naisbitt, Author

Q } What's in a plan? What does a good plan look like?

A } A strategic plan outlines where your organization wants to be – typically over a fixed period of time – and defines how you are going to get there. The word "**how**" is important. That's where the strategy comes in. It's easy to make a list of the things you want or need to achieve, but you must also understand how you're going to achieve them. To do otherwise is to leave the direction of your organization to chance.

The foundation of your strategic plan is your organization's vision and mission. As with everything you do, the plan should always tie back to these. It's likely that you've already formulated these, but if you haven't (say, if you're consulting this book as you consider launching a new organization), it's definitely the place to start.

A good strategic plan (either through a document or a collaborative strategic planning process) will spell out the goals everyone in the organization is seeking to achieve. From there, it'll identify the action steps necessary to achieve each goal. This includes the staff resources, time and financial support involved (along with where these will come from). As we dig deeper, a detailed timeline and budget will also be included and often a brief history of where the organization has been.

At the end of the day, your plan could be one, five or 100 pages. Truth be told, it might even be on one PowerPoint slide. What's most important is what you do with it. Ask yourself these questions:

▶ There's no prescribed format for a strategic plan, no right or wrong way of doing things. What matters most is not what your plan looks like, but what you do with it.

- Do your clients, staff and board understand the mission and vision?

- Have they all agreed upon the goals designed to achieve the mission and vision?

- Are they committed to executing the plan at every turn, externally and internally?

- Do they understand the steps necessary and resources required (time, money, etc.) to get the organization where it wants to be?

All of these are essential ingredients of a sound strategic plan. What the product itself looks like really doesn't matter as long as it reflects your organization's heart and soul.

NO. **3**

Q | Is it necessary or important to hire a consultant to do planning, or can we do it ourselves?

A There are many compelling reasons to hire a consultant. Perhaps you don't have the expertise to guide the strategic planning process on your own. The right consultant will have experience in your field and bring context to the table – based on his/ her experience – that may not be available to you independently. He or she can help facilitate a process so that all staff can participate, as well as offer an outside point of view that may very well yield some insights you haven't considered.

If you do consider a consultant, make sure he or she understands and has experience with the various planning models available, so that he or she can assist you in making the best choice for your nonprofit. A good consultant should be able to provide multiple examples of his or her work that have been tailored to the needs of nonprofit clients. You'll also want to make sure that a potential consultant's style and process are a good fit for your organization. Take your time and get to know the people you may be engaging.

That said, hiring outside help is not always practical or even possible for smaller nonprofits. That's one of the reasons we've developed this chapter. The decision to rely on internal vs. external resources should be made based on the availability of funds and the availability of in-kind support (such as a board member with expertise in this area).

If resources are particularly limited, you might consider hiring a consultant to facilitate and guide the process at fixed intervals (e.g., a board planning retreat). A trained facilitator can stimulate discussion and ask the right questions, while ensuring that the discourse remains objective and civil. He or she should also be willing to share observations about the discussion and thoughts on related implications. So, while a facilitator would not technically write the plan or implement the entire process, he or she is often in a position to jump in at just the right moment.

▶ If resources are limited, but you find you need outside help, consider hiring an independent facilitator to guide the planning process at fixed intervals (e.g., a board retreat).

Q | What's the purpose of the environmental scan and how do we get this? Is that the same thing as a SWOT analysis?

A } An environmental scan is an objective review of the current and anticipated environmental factors that impact your organization. These can include, for example, the political, economic and demographic environment in which you're operating.

A few other important areas to consider are: the regulatory environment, philanthropic and donor trends, and other organizations providing similar services or competing for the same funds. The latter point is often overlooked, but it's extremely important. You can use services like Charity Navigator (www.charitynavigator.org) to get a good sense of who is operating in your area and providing similar services. Keep in mind, this need not be a negative. You might find that someone is doing something complementary and you can actually enhance each other's work. Another place to gather intelligence is the Foundation Directory Online, a database of grantmakers and grantees (www.fconline.foundationcenter.org) developed by the Foundation Center. This is an efficient way to learn who's funding organizations like yours.

▸ Use online, print and government resources to fully understand the environment you're operating in. This will help to illuminate key trends, challenges and opportunities for your organization.

The environmental scan helps you to understand the broader context in which you're operating. By investing the time to identify key trends and environmental factors that impact your nonprofit, you can begin to think through the implications and, where appropriate, plan a course of action.

Organizations frequently choose only to look at the external factors, although a strong case can be made for considering your internal environment. This includes looking at your organization's internal capacities and resources, and projecting how those may need to change in the future to meet your objectives.

A SWOT analysis is derived from your environmental scan. "SWOT" stands for strengths, weaknesses, opportunities and threats. Identifying these can help to focus your scan's findings. For example, let's say you represent an organization that provides small loans to low-income entrepreneurs. Your environmental scan may reveal that a new regulation is being considered that changes how you track and report on beneficiaries. That's an objective observation in your scan. However, as you drill down into your SWOT analysis, you might note

No. 4

▶ When identifying
strengths and
weaknesses, focus
on areas that
indicate distinctive
characteristics (good
or bad) within your
organization, and that
can be acted upon.

that such a regulation would create privacy issues for your clients
or cost significant money to be in compliance. Those are identified
"threats" in your SWOT analysis.

Strengths and weaknesses tend to be associated with the internal
environment, or the situation inside the organization (operations,
performance quality, infrastructure, governance, etc.). These also
tend to be in the present. Opportunities and threats, therefore,
relate to the external environment – the situation outside of the
organization. These tend to be posited in the future (competition,
trends, political landscape, etc.).

When you conduct a SWOT analysis, be direct, be concrete and focus
on constructive observations. For example, under "strengths," it isn't
particularly useful to say your staff is committed to your mission.
Many nonprofits share that trait (although the opposite would
certainly be a weakness). Instead, focus on areas that indicate a
distinctiveness and that result in action. Here are a few examples
to stimulate your thinking:

- If yours is the only organization providing X and Y services within
  300 miles, that is probably a strength. The resulting action could
  be that you plan to expand services to the surrounding counties.

- A weakness could be that you rely too heavily on certain types
  of funding. A possible resulting action? Develop and implement
  a strategy to diversify fundraising.

- An infusion of new government funding aimed at your target
  audience and the services you provide would present an
  opportunity. In that event, you'd probably want to identify
  strategies to make your organization known amongst the
  decision-makers and, of course, apply for the funding.

While there are many consultants who specialize in this area of
analysis, many smaller organizations find they have little choice but
to go it alone. An excellent place to start is to consider your target
market. What, for example, is the current and projected population?
What trends affect your target audience as it relates to education,
health, income, employment, etc.?

Another useful component to the assessment phase is to survey
external stakeholders (e.g., funders, clients, community leaders,
etc.) about your organization. External perspectives on such issues
as your organization's greatest contributions, challenges observed,
anticipated (or missed) opportunities, and even basics like how

others would describe your organization, can lead to some surprising insights.

It should also be noted that the environmental scan and SWOT analysis should be key parts of the assessment phase.

There are many resources that can assist you in the development of an environmental scan. For example, government agencies such as the U.S. Census Bureau (www.census.gov) and Bureau of Labor Statistics (www.bls.gov) can serve as rich sources of demographic and economic data. Local United Way affiliates (www.liveunited.org) also produce periodic reports that offer valuable information to nonprofits. In addition, colleagues in your field should be able to provide valuable insights.

Of course, current and potential clients should also be tapped as key resources to understand subjective points of view regarding realities on the ground.

" First get your facts; then you can distort them at your leisure. "

- Mark Twain

Visit www.nonprofitanswerguide.org for timely sector resources and more expert answers to your most immediate nonprofit questions.

QUICK TIP

NO. **5**

Q › What does an organization assessment cover, when should it be done and how can it be helpful?

A › An organization assessment — also commonly referred to as an organizational audit, taking stock, or an information-gathering phase — lays the groundwork for your strategic plan related to your organization's capacity. As such, it should be conducted very early in the planning process. Its primary purpose is to help stakeholders understand the past and current state of your organization as a launching pad for thinking about the future.

A good starting place is to gather all relevant documentation — annual reports, program reports to funders, past strategic plans and assessments, financial reports, etc. Many strategic planners then recommend developing an assessment tool for use by those involved in the planning process.

An assessment tool is typically organized as a survey around various programmatic and functional areas such as:

- Human resources
- Legal
- Financial
- Fundraising
- Marketing and communications
- Specific major programs

▶ The organization assessment is the foundation of your strategic plan. After clarifying your vision and mission, it's the first thing you should do.

A common approach is to develop questions within each area that provide a snapshot as to how the organization is doing. For example, under a specific program, questions might include: "Do we have the resources committed to maintain the program?" and "Is the program in line with our mission?" Questions for the human resources category might ask, "Are we staffed at appropriate levels to carry out our goals?" or "Is staff compensation appropriate to industry standards?"

There are several organizations that offer free assessment tools to guide you in this process, including the Center for Nonprofit Excellence (www.cnpe.org) and Centerpoint for Leaders (www.centerpointforleaders.org).

The end product of this effort should be a report that lays out key findings and implications. Many of these will form the basis of your strategic plan.

Q How can we make sure the plan is realistic and doable?

A The first part of the answer may seem obvious, but give it serious consideration: Ask the people who are actually charged with executing the plan whether or not it's realistic. For example, plenty of people have been told to "create a viral video" without being given any direction as to its purpose, content or dissemination. Unless that staff person moonlights as a creative director at a leading ad agency, such a directive will fail.

While that is, we hope, an extreme example, your plan will likely include many expectations of the people who are working to advance your mission. Our advice? Engage them in the process and openly invite their feedback when action plans and timelines are established.

Another way to determine the feasibility of your strategic plan is to look at other organizations with similar missions and size that have achieved what you want to achieve. For media awareness, consider using Google Alerts (see question 10 for more information) to track others in your field and geographic area. In terms of fundraising, the Foundation Directory Online (www.fconline.foundationcenter.org) is a great resource to see how much other organizations have received, and from whom.

While crafting the strategies, be sure to build a budget for all of the costs and resources needed for each strategy. Many of the costs may be related to staff time, and realistic assessments of staff availability need to be made.

One caveat: It's not uncommon to hear a nonprofit of any size announce that it wants to be, for example, the next Susan G. Komen for the Cure. Komen is a case study to be sure, and a lofty goal for any nonprofit. But remember that reality is the key to executing your plan. Looking at organizations with far more resources than you have is only helpful in thinking about what you may want (or not want) in the future. The important thing is to understand who you are, and to establish standards based on that reality.

> ▶ Your plan will likely include many expectations of the people who are working to advance your mission. Our advice? Engage them in the process and openly invite their feedback when action plans and timelines are established.

Keep up with the conversation. Use Google Alerts to track web mentions and media coverage of others in your field or service area.

QUICK TIP

NO. 7

Q How do we strike a balance between visionary, out-of-the-box thinking and pragmatism?

A The easy answer? Be open to both.

Your strategic plan should make sense to the average person who cares about your issue. It should, therefore, be pragmatic in laying out goals, strategies and action plans. This can include all sorts of "standard" tools, including media, PR, fundraising and marketing, among many others.

At the same time, there should be plenty of room for out-of-the-box thinking. The implementation ideas you put forth in your plan are not cast in stone. The key is to be open to new ideas, test them and refine when appropriate. Not every idea will work, so it's important to be open to and learn from failure.

A collaborative process that invites and embraces new ideas is an important element in stimulating creative thinking. Build brainstorming into your planning experience and make it clear that all ideas are welcome.

Once you've decided on a direction, the big ideas can be made a lot more tangible by thinking through the practical steps that need to be taken to execute them. You might also find that it's helpful to break action steps down into phases. For example, a major ad campaign might be phased every six months as: preparation, research, fundraising, creative development, production, placement and evaluation. That's clearly an oversimplified example, but the point is that by outlining each of these six-month phases, you can assess how realistic your goals are, put a course of action into play, and help people to see how the big idea will actually unfold.

The most important thing to remember? You can't achieve big things unless you're open to the possibilities.

▸ A good plan will generate two thoughts. The first is, "Of course, that's exactly what we need." The second is, "Wow, that's a big idea." One calms, the other excites. Come up with a plan that elicits both, and you've found the balance.

Q How long a period should the plan cover?

A Strategic plans can cover anywhere from 0 to 10 years. The most common is a three-year timeframe, but the final decision depends on your needs. The three-year (or more) timeframe was at one time well-suited to an organization that knew exactly where it was headed and was not likely to be thrown off-course by technological advances or changes in the economy. We know now that very few of those organizations actually exist.

If you determine that the best course of action calls for a malleable plan that responds to in-the-moment needs, then you might be best served by a plan that establishes your vision and defines strategies that enable you to respond to issues in real-time. Such plans evolve constantly over time.

Other factors to consider are anticipated changes in the policy and economic environment in which you're operating. For example, let's say it's 2008 and you run a community health center. In 2009, the American Recovery and Reinvestment Act (more commonly referred to as the "stimulus") allocated $2 billion in extra funding for such centers. This was anticipated well in advance. If your organization was a strong candidate for this funding, you would have needed a strategic plan flexible enough to respond to the opportunity.

The larger point is that flexibility is of critical importance to any strategic plan, regardless of the timeframe it covers. There will always be changes that can't be anticipated – some positive (such as the launch of a large new foundation in your service area) and some negative (such as a rise in unemployment). Likewise, unforeseen opportunities are likely to present themselves (e.g., a speaking invitation at a major conference or a high-profile media request). Your plan must anticipate that some things can't be anticipated, and offer a system for taking advantage of them.

Also keep in mind that once plans are developed, it's important to review them regularly to assess your progress, regardless of the timeframe you've outlined. Many organizations choose to do this quarterly. For example, you might begin the quarter by reviewing what has been accomplished in the prior 90 days, aligning these developments with your overall goals, and laying out where you expect to be 90 days from now. This information should also be tied to the metrics outlined in your plan so you can assess progress regularly.

▶ There are no rules on the timeframe. It could be three, five or ten years. Or, your plan could be a constantly evolving tool that has no timeline attached. Either way, flexibility is of critical importance. There will always be changes that can't be anticipated, so you must be able to adapt. Also remember to review your plans regularly to assess progress and any need for refinements.

No. **9**

Q We already know what we want to do, why do we need to spend all this time and effort on planning? OR ... Our funders tell us what and how they want us to operate, so why do we need to plan?

A It's not unusual for the strategic planning process to reveal that key stakeholders have different ideas about "what we want to do." A strategic plan helps to build consensus and clarity on the organization's mission, values and goals. Also, you may very well find that the planning effort stimulates new thinking and strengthens organization-wide collaboration.

Importantly, knowing what you want to do says nothing about how you're going to do it, nor does it take into account the external factors that are likely to impact your activities. This is the job of your strategic plan. When it's done well, the plan will serve as a rallying point for everyone involved in your organization and focus them on the end goal: accomplishing the mission.

Responding to the wishes of your funders is not a substitute for strategic planning. While it's very likely that your budget includes restricted funds that are tied to a donor's requirements, this shouldn't define your overall strategy. A strategic plan charts a course of action for your whole organization. It also helps you to identify the characteristics of programs and activities that are the right fit for your vision and mission. Ultimately, your plan should increase your odds for impact and sustainability. There's no substitute for it.

An important function of your strategic plan: to make sure your stakeholders understand and buy into your organization's mission, values and goals.

QUICK TIP

Q | How can we effectively track whether we're achieving our goals or not? Who should do this?

A | A strategic plan should have measurable outcomes (or "metrics") as a key component of content. These will vary widely depending on your goals, but a few common measures include:

- Increased number of clients served.

- Lower cost per service.

- Increased revenues from fee-for-service.

- Increased percentage of clients transitioning from the program due to self-sufficiency.

- Increased media mentions.

- Growth in monthly website users, time on site, pages/downloads accessed, etc.

- Increased awareness in the community served or among specific target populations.

- Growth in corporate sponsorships.

- Number of policymakers briefed on objective research and analysis.

Whatever your metrics, your plan should establish realistic goals over time that can easily be referred to and assessed. For example, an online education provider might seek to have a 10 percent increase in users requesting more information over six months, and a 20 percent increase in the conversion rate (meaning that 20 percent more people seeking information ultimately subscribe as compared to today). If the provider has laid out strategies to achieve that (e.g., through marketing, advertising, social media campaigns, etc.), then these may well be realistic goals. And, these are easy, cost-efficient and realistic to measure (for more information, see Chapter 8: Evaluation).

▶ Measurable goals are central to any strategic plan. Planned actions should be aligned with clear and realistic metrics, along with a plan on how you will capture data.

No. 10

The individuals responsible for measuring your progress are likely to vary. For example, those involved in online marketing would measure web analytics, while development staff would report on sponsorships, and finance specialists would be best positioned to track trends in fees for service.

Of course, a smaller nonprofit may not have the benefit of dedicated staff for each of these functions. Fortunately, there are still plenty of cost-effective tools available to you, such as:

- Your bookkeeper (even if it's you) should be able to run reports on financial metrics from standard bookkeeping software such as QuickBooks or Peachtree.

▶ Once you've established realistic metrics, they aren't usually that difficult to track. The real key is to establish a system to track them regularly. Doing so will be of great benefit to measuring the success of your strategic plan and it will also make reporting to funders incredibly easy when the time comes.

- Awareness and program quality can be measured through in-person and online surveys (SurveyMonkey™ – **www.surveymonkey.com** – is one free resource) and discussion groups conducted at your facility.

- Google Analytics (**www.google.com/intl/en/analytics**) is a free service that allows for a detailed analysis of your Web traffic, including, among other things, numbers of users (new and returning), where they are from and how they are getting there.

- Google Alerts (**www.google.com/alerts**) sends free real-time email updates of media and Web mentions of keywords you set.

❝ Everything that can be counted does not necessarily count; everything that counts cannot necessarily be counted. ❞

- Albert Einstein

Web analytics, online survey tools and media tracking websites can be great tools to measure your progress. Better yet, many of them are free.

QUICK TIP

TOOLS FOR NONPROFIT PLANNING

- **Center for Nonprofit Excellence**
  (www.cnpe.org)

- **Centerpoint for Leaders**
  (www.centerpointforleaders.org)

- **Independent Sector's Charting Impact**
  (www.independentsector.org/charting_impact)

DATA GATHERING AND TREND ANALYSIS

- **Bureau of Labor Statistics**
  (www.bls.gov)

- **CDC National Center for Health Statistics**
  (www.cdc.gov/nchs)

- **National Center for Education Statistics**
  (www.nces.ed.gov)

- **United Way Worldwide**
  (www.liveunited.org)

- **U.S. Census Bureau**
  (www.census.gov)

STRATEGIC PLANNING CONSULTANTS

- **Center for Nonprofit Management**
  (www.cnmsocal.org)

MEASUREMENT TOOLS

- **Google Alerts**
  (www.google.com/alerts)

- **Google Analytics**
  (www.google.com/intl/en/analytics)

- **SurveyMonkey™**
  (www.surveymonkey.com)

READY-TO-GO-RESOURCES

20-SECOND-SUMMARY

- The strategic planning process is as important as the plan itself. Approach it as a way to galvanize staff and leadership around common goals and chart a course of action together.

- There's no right or wrong way to do a plan. There's only what's right for your organization. Take the time to familiarize yourself with different models and approaches. Then decide what's best suited to your resources and organizational culture.

- Great plans aren't created in a vacuum. Engage your board and key staff every step of the way. If they don't believe in the plan, no one will.

- Be sure to establish realistic metrics and track them regularly. This will help you to gauge how you're doing and understand where refinements will be necessary.

- No time to read this chapter? Here are some common steps in the planning process:
    1. Identify the mission and vision.
    2. Conduct an environmental scan, SWOT analysis and organizational assessment.
    3. Identify the goals, strategies and tactics.
    4. Write the plan.
    5. Develop an income and expense budget.
    6. Implement the plan.

8

EVALUATION

If you've been in the business of running a nonprofit for a while, you've probably noticed increasing emphasis on evaluation.

In the face of declining resources, your donors, the media, government and the public all want to know what's working and the impact of your endeavors. There's a good chance you do too. Evaluation can be a great tool to demonstrate the value of your programs.

So what's the hold up? If yours is like a lot of nonprofits, the concerns probably have to do with money, time, internal buy-in and, yes, apprehension about the results.

This chapter offers advice to overcome these obstacles. We'll walk through the basic steps of evaluation planning, clarify some buzzwords you've been hearing (perhaps we can interest you in a logic model?) and help you think through the roles of staff, board and outside consultants.

This chapter provides a top-level look at evaluation. It's meant for those who are just starting to consider evaluation's role in programming. We offer plenty of resources to help you dig deeper. By the end, we hope you'll come to see that evaluation need not be scary; it's just a tool to inform decision-making and maximize efficiency and impact. And really, what change-seeker doesn't want that?

Q } What is an evaluation plan? Why should I create one?

A } An evaluation plan is a roadmap that identifies the goals and ways in which you'll collect and analyze data. This includes which information you'll collect, along with how, where and when you'll collect it. It identifies your research methods, those responsible for carrying out the plan, timelines and budget, and should include how the information will be shared and used.

One of the most important aspects of your plan is articulating the questions that the evaluation will be structured to answer. Frequently this will relate to both outputs (e.g., the specifics of what is being done – services provided, number of people served) and outcomes (i.e., the actual change that resulted from the program).

For example, let's say you run a technology training program for at-risk youth. Output-oriented questions might look at the number of trainings conducted, number of people served, retention rates, and things like meetings with community leaders or policymakers. Questions geared toward outcomes might measure beneficiaries' increase in skills, changed attitudes, behavior changes, etc.

The number one reason you should create an evaluation plan is because you want to deliver the very best programs and services. An evaluation plan helps you to refine your data collection and assessment practices so that the information you glean is most useful to advancing your mission and the objectives of the program. It also helps to establish a culture of evaluation within your organization whereby people are always thinking about how to make sure the necessary information is being gathered to improve programs.

Evaluation results can also be extremely useful communications tools that help you more efficiently respond to your funders' needs. They can be significant credibility builders that increase your capacity to raise funds for the program.

▶ Need help identifying appropriate outcomes for your program? The Center for What Works (www.whatworks.org) has teamed up with the Urban Institute to develop recommended indicators for nonprofits working in 14 different issue areas.

The purpose of an evaluation plan is to help guide your organization toward the most feasible and useful evaluation possible. The right planning now means more efficient, more effective programs later.

QUICK TIP

No. **2**

Q ⟩ **What is the difference between process, outcome and impact evaluations?**

> ▶ A process evaluation basically tells you whether a program rolled out as planned and reached the intended target audience. Outcome and impact evaluations go further in that they tell you what kind of change resulted from the program, both for your target audience and at a deeper societal level.

A ⟩ A process evaluation looks at the actual development and implementation of a particular program. It establishes whether you've hit quantifiable targets and implemented strategies as planned. It's typically done throughout the program to allow for mid-course corrections and continuous quality improvement. This type of evaluation can be very useful in determining how to improve all aspects of program delivery.

While they can be done separately, outcome and impact evaluations are important additions to a process evaluation. Outcome evaluation measures the change that has occurred as a result of a program. For example, your process evaluation might confirm that 200 people have completed your skills-training program. An outcome evaluation would tell you how many of those demonstrated increased confidence, changed behaviors, found jobs because of new skills, etc.

An impact evaluation looks at the long-term, deeper changes that have resulted from that program. This type of evaluation could, for example, suggest that the behavior changes to your participants' lives continued over time and perhaps transferred across generations.

While the outcome evaluation tells us what kind of change has occurred, an impact evaluation paints a picture as to how a program might have affected participants' lives on a broader scale.

It's important to note that certain types of evaluation are more involved than others. For example, while certain outcomes can be easily and reliably measured, true impact measurement is a much trickier business. In its truest sense, impact and outcome measurement often involves using an independent evaluator, establishing control groups, and measuring changes over extended periods of time. This can be extremely costly, and reliable results may take years to emerge (depending on the nature of the program, of course).

We raise these issues not to sway you from impact evaluation. Rather, we want to paint a complete-enough picture to encourage you to invest the resources when the time is right. In other words, if your program's content is potentially replicable and highly impactful – an HIV prevention program or a curriculum intended to connect young adults to good jobs, for example – then it's probably worth it to find the necessary funding to have it evaluated at full scale.

Q Why all the hype about logic models?

A A program logic model is an important component of evaluation planning because it helps you to identify the most relevant evaluation questions. It shows both what the program is supposed to do and how its components will lead to outcomes.

There's probably more "hype" around the term than the idea. In fact, there's a good chance you're already using a logic model and just haven't put it down on paper yet. Logic models are often presented in complex terms, but the concept itself isn't that complicated. At its most basic level, a logic model is a graphic or roadmap that shows how your program is intended to work. It depicts a linear path from your assumptions to your process, to expected outcomes and impact.

The W.K. Kellogg Foundation describes a basic logic model as a pathway that starts with resources/inputs and then moves toward activities, outputs, outcomes and finally, impact.

Fortunately, there are a lot of free resources to help nonprofits develop a program logic model. The Kellogg Foundation's freely available *Logic Model Development Guide* and Innovation Network's free online *Logic Model Builder* can be extremely useful to anyone looking for assistance in this area. Importantly, both of these resources offer guidance and tools to help nonprofits connect the logic model to an evaluation plan.

It's important to note that the process of developing an effective logic model will require some thought and preparation. For organizations looking for guidance through that process, the Center for Nonprofit Management provides training and coaching opportunities to help make the most of available tools. For more information, visit **www.cnmsocal.org** and click on the "Consulting & Coaching" tab.

▶ A logic model is a linear path that describes how your program expects to go from a hypothesis to action to outcomes. The exercise of creating one is an important part of evaluation planning because it helps you determine the key questions the evaluation will answer.

You don't have to do it all alone! Be sure to check out the range of available resources out there to help you build your organization's logic model.

QUICK TIP

NO. **4**

Q } **What makes a good evaluation?**

A } The Joint Committee on Standards for Educational Evaluation (www.jcsee.org) has defined four main principles that underlie good evaluation:

1. **UTILITY:** This ensures that the evaluation is collecting credible, useful, timely information. The purpose of an evaluation is to determine what works and how, and to inform decision-making so it addresses current needs and realities.

2. **FEASIBILITY:** This principle prioritizes evaluation that is practical, cost-effective and politically viable.

3. **PROPRIETY:** This relates to legal and ethical standards that should govern an evaluation, including careful consideration of those involved as well as those who might be impacted by the results.

4. **ACCURACY:** The data yielded must be accurate to be useful (and ensure credibility). This is connected to the rigor of your evaluation plan, data collection methods and willingness to report both the good and bad.

Adapted in part from the *Joint Committee on Standards for Educational Evaluation's "Program Evaluation Standards Statements."*

As much as it might be tempting to focus on only the positive, doing so erodes credibility. Most donors, and people in general, understand that failure is instructive. For a nonprofit, it can lead to the refinement or refocus that ultimately creates positive change. On the other hand, you'd be hard-pressed to find anyone understanding of an organization that swept negative findings under the rug. Finally, good evaluation design flows from your logic model. Since your logic model explains how you'll create change, the evaluation is linked to it in that it'll confirm where you are on target and what needs to be refined.

USEFUL EVALUATION GUIDELINES

▸ Be sure program components can realistically be evaluated.

▸ Build on available research.

▸ Choose measures that fit what you're doing and follow standards for credible assessment.

▸ Observe ethical standards for the fair treatment of study participants.

▸ Measure both process and outcome.

▸ Report both positive and negative results.

▸ Share results to maximize their value.

Adapted from: *Principles of Sound Impact Evaluation* (www.fns.usda.gov)

Q | What are the basic responsibilities of the board, and of individual board members, regarding evaluation?

A | Ensuring the effectiveness of a nonprofit's programs is among a board of directors' chief responsibilities. Effective evaluation helps the board carry out that duty. The board's specific level of involvement, however, depends on a number of factors, including the organization's size, the scale and potential impact of the evaluation, and staff capacity.

A board member has a responsibility to determine your organization's internal capacity for evaluation and assess the financial feasibility of the evaluation plan. From there, he or she might be involved in everything from monitoring, planning and ensuring that the right questions are being asked, to confirming the objectivity and integrity of the results. For a smaller organization where evaluations are not the norm, the board should review the evaluation plan, provide input as it's refined, and ultimately authorize the plan. However, this is likely impractical for a large organization, where involvement may be limited to reviewing findings.

Given the board's role in guiding and authorizing the programmatic direction of an organization, evaluation results should be of utmost interest to the members collectively and individually. These help board members to understand whether the organization is meeting its goals; the results also help them to set strategic priorities.

An individual board member's specific role in evaluation will likely be determined by his or her interest level and expertise. For example, if you're fortunate enough to have a board member with a background in research methods, you'll likely want to actively engage this individual in evaluation planning. Your board chair will also have an important role to play in terms of championing the evaluation plan and explaining the board's role to individual members.

It's also important for the executive director to communicate with the board members and establish clear expectations around their role in evaluation. Many executive directors are surprised to find that their expectations are not necessarily in line with what the board expects, so good communication is essential.

▸ Understanding what works and what doesn't is central to a nonprofit board's decision-making process. That's why the board should be involved in the evaluation process every step of the way — from reviewing, refining and authorizing the plan, to utilizing results to set the strategic direction.

NO.
6

Q } **How can we justify spending resources on evaluation when our budget is so tight?**

A } This is a common issue facing nonprofits of all sizes. The reality, however, is that a properly executed evaluation can actually save your organization money — or at least bring in more of it — in the long-run. For example, let's say you run a program that delivers low-cost food to those who need it, but you've experienced a lack of return beneficiaries, which are critical to your revenue stream.

You could assume that attrition is the result of reduced need, but that's unlikely. An evaluation could reveal that your hours are not meeting the end-users' needs. In that case, you might just change your hours. Alternatively, you might find that the products you offer aren't meeting their needs, your services are duplicative of another organization's, or that your intake process is too time-consuming. All of these can be easily remedied, but you won't know what to fix if you don't evaluate.

In addition, reliable evaluation results can serve as an important PR tool and may boost your credibility in the eyes of funders. You might also find that philanthropic funders are willing to include a line-item in your budget to enable you to effectively evaluate the program they're funding. An evaluation is frequently of great interest to funders as it allows them to understand whether and how their investments are having the greatest impact. These are among the reasons that many funders' grant proposal formats require that you indicate how you will measure impact.

▶ Done properly, evaluation can provide valuable insights to make your services more efficient and cost-effective. In other words, the benefits can easily outweigh the costs.

Q · There is a great deal of resistance in our organization toward evaluation; what can we do?

A · Internal resistance to evaluation is a common issue for many nonprofit organizations. It could be that staff feel the program is moving along just fine so evaluation is seen as a waste of precious time. Other frequent concerns are that the evaluation findings might result in a discontinued program, lost jobs or an increased workload. Sometimes resistance is related to staff insecurities and lack of experience with evaluation.

Strong internal communication and early involvement are the keys to generating the internal buy-in necessary to carry out an effective evaluation. Be candid about the purpose of the evaluation and your team's role in carrying it out. Don't be afraid to address the hard questions (e.g., "What if the findings are negative?"), and above all, stress the evaluation's role in advancing your mission and program objectives. To increase comfort levels and fully engage your staff, invite them to ask questions and provide suggestions about the evaluation. Consider establishing a system that invites this input anonymously so your staff can raise issues that might be considered sensitive. Also keep in mind that devoting staff meetings to training and/or engaging a consultant to provide technical assistance can help allay fears and move the process forward.

It's also very likely that your program staff will be involved in data collection. They may, for example, be responsible for completing intake forms or administering pre- and post-service surveys. It's critical that staff understand the importance of these activities and their relationship to program planning, refinement and continued funding. To that end, it's important to build internal capacity for evaluation. Key staff need to understand, feel confident and have a good working knowledge of evaluation to support the effort and contribute effectively. If you aren't completely comfortable in this capacity-building role, consider engaging an expert in the area.

Finally, take steps to ensure that staff are comfortable with their roles, have the opportunity to ask questions and suggest refinements, and are involved in the design process. After all, your program staff are often in the best position to know what information can be gleaned from your beneficiaries.

▶ Resistance to evaluation is common, but not insurmountable. Communicate with your staff openly and engage them in the planning process to ensure that concerns are addressed and their perspectives are integrated into the plan.

Q We already collect a lot of information for our funders that is not helpful to us. How can we prevent ourselves from drowning in useless information?

A At some time or another, most nonprofit executives have been involved in collecting data required by their funders that they feel doesn't benefit the program or its clients. While the nonprofit sector will likely never be completely free of onerous data collection requirements, an evaluation plan can help you to build on what's required in a way that is beneficial to your mission.

For example, let's say you run a mentoring program and your funder requires demographic data regarding your beneficiaries. This will most certainly involve some kind of standard data collection method, such as an intake form. Now let's assume that you're more interested in knowing whether your beneficiaries are performing better in school. You might modify the intake form to gather baseline information about student performance and then do an annual survey to track changes. (Note: This is a cursory example to demonstrate how a data collection requirement might be modified. In this example, and most others, a lot of other factors would need to be addressed – such as a control group, in this example – to generate reliable data.)

You might also find that engaging your funder(s) in evaluation planning yields valuable insights (program officers at large foundations often have experience in evaluation), builds the relationship, and presents an opportunity to identify evaluation questions that serve the funder and the program. For example, question 1 of this chapter talks about measurement of **outputs** and **outcomes**. Outputs are required by funders, as are outcomes which address the meaningful change that has occurred. By engaging your funders in a dialogue on outcomes, you're opening up the lines of communication to establish a system that benefits everyone.

▶ Where it's practical, try to build on what's already required of you in a way that serves your evaluation plan. If funder requirements have caused you to implement certain data collection techniques, consider how you can augment those to gather the data you need.

Q | Do we have to evaluate everything? How do we choose, given our limited resources?

A For an organization with only one main program, the answer is easy: Yes, evaluate the program. However, things are quite a bit more complicated for those with multiple programs and especially multiple locations. In an ideal world, you'd be able to evaluate all of your programs. Economic realities being what they are, however, this may not be possible right away. Following are some criteria to consider when determining which programs or parts of a program to place at the top of the list:

- Anything that might be considered a signature program or represents a growth area for your organization.

- Work that is (or should be) in a growth stage and appears especially promising.

- Programs that reach relatively large numbers of people.

- Those with relatively large budgets (as a percentage of your overall budget).

- Programs that, when evaluated, have the potential to demonstrate the importance of your mission and approach.

- Those that can potentially be scaled in other communities or otherwise inform the broader field of practice.

- Programs that funders require be evaluated.

▶ If you're not in a position to evaluate all of your programs just yet, try starting with your signature programs – the ones that reach the most people, have the highest awareness and can demonstrate your mission most effectively.

The Colorado Nonprofit Association (**www.coloradononprofits.org**) suggests that nonprofits consider piloting an evaluation approach in one or two programs before rolling it out organization-wide. This enables the organization to better understand the time and financial implications associated with evaluation, as well as determine whether the evaluation is actually yielding the information it wants.

Consider piloting your evaluation approach on select programs before expanding it throughout the organization. This will allow you to refine your approach and make sure you're prepared to conduct the evaluation.

QUICK TIP

NO. 10

Q | Do we need a consultant to help us?

A | Using the services of a consultant can be beneficial in several instances, such as when you don't have the necessary expertise or time, when you'll benefit from an objective point of view (and one could argue that this is always the case), or when it's required by a funder.

To the latter point, some government and philanthropic funding will require an independent evaluation. In that case, the donor institution will likely select – or at least approve – the evaluation consultant. If this is the case, consider yourself lucky and push for the most rigorous evaluation possible. Your organization and your field will be better for it.

▶ While it's not always possible for nonprofits to hire one, an independent consultant can add a lot of value in terms of expertise and objectivity.

If you do decide to utilize the services of a consultant, there are many resources available to help you select the right one. For example, the American Evaluation Association (www.eval.org) offers a list of member evaluators by location and areas of expertise. You might also consider asking trusted colleagues and others in your field for recommendations. For organizations located in Southern California, the Center for Nonprofit Management (www.cnmsocal.org) provides consulting services, trainings and workshops to help guide you through this process.

It's reasonable to expect potential consultants to develop a proposal that outlines their experience, approach to the project, past work samples, references and budget. Soliciting proposals from several evaluators will help you to understand the range of possibilities and enable you and your board to make a fully informed decision. You'll also want to interview candidates with your board to ensure that the evaluator you choose is a good match for your organization's style and culture.

One final note: A good consultant can also serve an important role in helping your staff and board understand the basic principles of evaluation and the role it plays in carrying out your work. To that end, organizations often find it helpful to build in an internal education component (e.g., a special meeting or brown-bag lunch that addresses the topic and answers questions) to the consultant's scope of work.

Need help choosing a consultant?
Visit www.managementhelp.org/staffing/consulting.htm for step-by-step tips.

QUICK TIP

TOOLS FOR EVALUATION PLANNING

- **The Center for What Works**
  (www.whatworks.org)

- **Innovation Network**
  (www.innonet.org)

- **Online Evaluation Resource Library**
  (www.oerl.sri.com)

- **W.K. Kellogg Foundation**
  (www.wkkf.org, search "evaluation")

EVALUATION CONSULTANTS

- **American Evaluation Association**
  (www.eval.org)

- **Center for Nonprofit Management**
  (www.cnmsocal.org)

TOOLS FOR BOARDS

- **BoardSource**
  (www.boardsource.org)

OVERVIEWS AND DEFINITIONS

- **Free Management Library**
  (www.managementhelp.org)

- **GrantSpace**
  (www.grantspace.org)

READY-TO-GO-RESOURCES

20-SECOND-SUMMARY

- Your board and staff should be actively engaged in the evaluation planning process. In addition to needing their buy-in, these key internal stakeholders are valuable sources of information and insight.

- Be sure to establish outcome indicators (i.e., the things you will measure to indicate change) that are realistic, measurable and will result in information that you can act upon in service to your mission.

- Evaluations are a good thing. Yes, they require time and money, but they also provide you with the information you need to deliver more effectively on your mission.

- Resist the urge to track only what would be considered positive results. Doing so erodes the credibility of your evaluation and organization. Besides, every organization — no matter how great — has room for improvement.

- In the last decade, donors have become ever more interested in evaluating the programs they fund. This also means that they've funded the development of tools that will help you in your efforts. Use them.

- Evaluation is a mindset that must exist throughout an organization, not just from the top-down. Everyone involved in designing and implementing programs should be thinking about how data can make those programs better.

9

MANAGING PEOPLE

30-SECOND-OVERVIEW

The strength of any nonprofit relies primarily on the strength of its people.

These are the folks who carry out your mission day in and day out. In most cases, they need to be motivated by a lot more than money (because let's face it, you probably don't have a lot). But how do you find people who are as passionate about your work as you are?

The question is actually more complicated than it might seem. First, you need to get very specific about what you mean by "people." Federal and state laws dictate whether an employee is exempt from overtime laws or not, and what makes a consultant a consultant. On top of that, there's a lot to know about recruiting, managing and being liable for volunteers. It's all very serious stuff.

This chapter provides an overview of how to define, recruit, manage and compensate various types of personnel. We'll take a look at tough disciplinary questions, along with strategies to find candidates who are the best match for your organization. This will help to jumpstart your process; but remember that laws vary drastically from state to state, so you'll need to be fully up to speed on what's required where you're operating.

DISCLAIMER: The information contained in this book is general in nature and may not be applicable to all situations. In addition, laws change. You should refer to the most current editions of additional resources listed for each topic and consult with a qualified human resources specialist and/or attorney on important matters.

Q How can we recruit employees for our organization?

A In the nonprofit sector, where salaries are often modest and resources are usually stretched thin, an organization's success depends in large part on the diverse skills, experience, flexibility and commitment of its workforce. But how do you find passionate candidates who have the skills you need to reach your constituency?

Today, most job seekers start by searching the Internet for advertised positions. This makes the web an effective way to reach out to a wide pool of potential candidates. But if you're looking for applicants keenly interested in the nonprofit sector, you'll want to advertise on sites targeted specifically to this audience.

To reach mission-driven, experienced nonprofit professionals, contact the Center for Nonprofit Management (CNM) to advertise in their job site, Nonprofit Jobs Cooperative (**www.nonprofitjobscoop. org**), which connects nonprofit employers and jobseekers. Other useful resources include Idealist (**www.idealist.org**), Opportunity Knocks (**www.opportunityknocks.org**) and The Chronicle of Philanthropy jobs section (**www.philanthropy.com**).

And don't forget to use the power of referrals. Let employees, colleagues, board members and professional associations know you're actively looking for qualified candidates and ask for recommendations. Studies show that most job seekers will ultimately find a position through a personal network.

TO FIND QUALIFIED APPLICANTS:

▸ Clearly articulate the position requirements.

▸ Use targeted methods of recruitment, such as nonprofit-specific websites.

▸ Reach out to associates and partner organizations to provide recommendations.

Always post opportunities on your website, Facebook page and LinkedIn!

QUICK TIP

2

Q | What's included in the hiring process?

A | Your organization is growing and it's time to recruit new employees. And chances are, you've decided to do the hiring yourself. But you're unsure of how to go about it. Follow these easy steps to help ensure a smooth and successful hiring process.

1. DEVELOP A CLEAR JOB DESCRIPTION. First, determine what you're looking for and put it down on paper. This will become your job description. The details should ideally be developed by a department supervisor, but you may also want to ask staff in the department to contribute.

Be sure to include:

- Job title and reporting structure.

- The purpose of the position and its relation to the organization's structure.

- Overall responsibilities, decision-making authority, and typical daily activities.

- Required skills, knowledge, education and experience.

- A bit of background about the organization.

2. ADVERTISE THE POSITION. Post on targeted websites, in community newsletters and on your website. Use social media tools such as Facebook and LinkedIn. Ask staff, colleagues and associates for recommendations. Use all avenues to get the word out about your open position.

3. REVIEW THE RESUMES. Digging through resumes for a qualified applicant can be an arduous task, so here are some tips to help speed the process:

- Before looking at resumes, review your job description and jot down the key skills and experience you need. Then, compare each resume to your list. Look for keywords and phrases that match.

- Pull viable candidates and review experience continuity. Look for gaps in employment history. If a candidate looks worthy, make notes directly on his or her resume for future review before and during an interview.

- If you have too many solid candidates, consider conducting preliminary interviews by phone to narrow down your list.

▶ Interviewing and unsure what you can or can't ask? Consult an attorney or reputable employment law guidebook covering both state and federal law.

4. CONSIDER HAVING QUALIFIED CANDIDATES COMPLETE AN EMPLOYMENT APPLICATION FORM. Once you identify promising candidates, you may want to have each applicant fill out a standard application form. Standardizing applications will enable you to quickly compare candidates, identify weaknesses or gaps in work history, and collect additional information that may not be in a resume. It will also help you tailor interviews for efficiency and avoid interview questions that may be sensitive or illegal.

5. INTERVIEW QUALIFIED CANDIDATES. In an interview, you'll want to be sure to ask about relevant skills and experience, nonprofit-specific training, and the candidate's motivation for seeking employment with your organization. To gauge knowledge about the sector and specific interest in your organization, ask about sector-specific challenges and what the candidate knows about your organization's history and mission. To make sure the candidate is a fit with your organization's values, ask what he or she looks for in a position and organizational culture.

▶ If you use a firm to run background checks, under the law you must disclose this to the applicant. The firm you choose can usually provide you with necessary forms.

It's important to note that when you hire an employee, you cannot discriminate on the basis of age, race, national origin, religion, gender, sexual orientation, disability and in some cases, veteran status. Therefore, understanding your interviewing responsibilities — what topics are sensitive or off-limits in an interview — is paramount.

6. CONDUCT REFERENCE CHECKS. As a prospective employer, you want to obtain a reference that clarifies an applicant's strengths and limitations. So, be sure to ask former employers about the candidate's job function, attitude and dependability, ability to take responsibility, relationships with co-workers and advancement potential.

Keep in mind, to protect against lawsuits, employers you contact may limit the scope of their reference to date of employment, job title and compensation level. If you're not getting enough information from HR or managers, consider asking the applicant to supply other references such as a co-worker or colleague and don't be afraid to reach out to your professional networks.

7. DRAFT A LETTER OFFERING EMPLOYMENT. Once you've chosen a candidate, you're going to want to write an offer of employment. This is a document that both you and the applicant will sign. The letter should include confirmation of title, compensation, employment status, job classification, description of benefits, first date of employment, orientation period (if any) and supervisor's name and title. If you're unsure, refer to a reputable hiring guide for tips and boilerplate language.

Q What do I need to know about classifying employees? What's the difference between an independent contractor and an employee?

A To fulfill their missions and make the most out of limited resources, more and more nonprofits are hiring a mix of employees and independent contractors. But classifying employees and determining who is and is not an independent contractor isn't always an easy task. If a hire is misclassified, an organization can face hefty fines and even lawsuits. So understanding the determining factors to classification is key. Here are the basics:

EMPLOYEES

To avoid paying overtime, an employer may be tempted to classify an employee as "exempt" under both federal and state law. (Non-exempt employees are entitled to overtime pay under the Fair Labor and Standards Act [FLSA], typically when they work more than 40 hours in a week.) Employees who might fall into this category include executive, administrative, and professional workers.

BEFORE YOU HIRE, KNOW THE BUSINESS RELATIONSHIP THAT EXISTS!

▶ Read IRS Publication 15-A: Employer's Supplemental Tax Guide. www.irs.gov/publications/p15a

But simply calling an employee a manager, or paying them a salary as opposed to an hourly rate, doesn't necessarily make an employee exempt. So do your research before making a classification. If you're unsure, it's best to refer to a reputable employment guide, an HR management firm or an attorney.

INDEPENDENT CONTRACTORS

The IRS, California courts and state agencies use a number of factors to determine whether an individual is an independent contractor or an employee. But because no single factor is conclusive on its own, it's sometimes difficult for hiring organizations to determine a relationship.

In general, independent contractors work on specific, time-bound projects and are able to work when, where and how they choose. For example, they wouldn't be required to work a set number of hours or onsite, to complete a job. They're usually paid by the project or on commission, as opposed to employees who may be paid by the hour or the month. They typically use their own equipment, work for more than one employer at a time, and their work is generally not integral to the continuation of business. Contractors are also responsible for satisfactory completion of a job or are legally obligated to make good for failure to complete it, allowing for profit or loss. To learn more, visit the IRS website (www.irs.gov).

Q | What should be included in a personnel policy?

A Developing documented policies and procedures is an essential step toward structuring an organization, guiding consistent and fair decision-making and ensuring a safe and happy workplace. Writing a personnel policy will help you establish a company culture and rules of conduct and help you determine how to handle situations before they arise. Once developed, it will also become the first resource you'll turn to when orienting a new employee.

A personnel policy can provide all kinds of details that your new, and established employees should know. It's up to you to decide how specific you want to get. Just remember, you're bound by the policy you create. So make sure it's not more restrictive than necessary by law. You may even want to talk to an employment lawyer to ask about labor rules that may affect you.

At minimum, your policy should contain discussion in the following areas:

ORIENTATION OR TRIAL PERIODS

Employers often use orientation or trial periods to apply an initial review of an employee or to phase in eligibility for benefits. If you choose to apply orientation or trial periods to new employees, be clear when and how their status will change, and seek legal advice if you're unsure.

SAFETY

As an employer, you're responsible for providing a safe workplace that meets health and safety standards. You must ensure employees are informed about hazardous chemicals and receive adequate safety training. You must also keep detailed safety records and notify the government about workplace accidents.

With this in mind, California law requires employers to develop an Illness and Injury Prevention Program. This policy should identify those responsible in your organization for implementing the Program,

UNSURE ABOUT SAFETY?

▸ Reach out to your insurance carrier or risk management expert to help identify potential problems.

It's always a good idea to have an attorney who is familiar with labor law review your personnel policy before you make it active policy.

QUICK TIP

NO. 4

and describe your system for identifying workplace hazards, correcting issues, communicating with and training staff, and ensuring Program compliance.

For more information on your workplace safety responsibilities, visit the Occupational Safety and Health Administration (OSHA) website (www.osha.gov).

HARASSMENT

It's your responsibility to create and enforce a harassment-free workplace. A comprehensive harassment policy can help you do that. A good policy takes a no-tolerance approach. It outlines types of harassment, describes prohibitive behavior, outlines training and education procedures, encourages victim reporting and ensures confidentiality. It also details complaint procedures, and promises prompt disciplinary action.

GRIEVANCE PROCEDURES

▸ If an employee reports harassment, under no circumstances should you do nothing — even if the employee requests that no action be taken. If you need advice about how to respond, consult a lawyer.

Though grievance procedures are not required by law, you may want to consider adding them to your personnel policy. Formal grievance procedures will boost employee confidence and provide specific steps for filing and responding to complaints. Developing policy in this area and consistently following it can save time and administrative costs when grievances do arise, and even minimize your exposure to liability.

When writing your grievance procedures, be specific about:

- Eligible employee classifications.
- The kinds of disputes that are covered.
- The steps to filing, and any time constraints.
- Levels of authority and the designation of substitutes.
- Rules governing evidence and cross-examination.
- Representation at grievance procedures and the use of arbitration.
- Any rules against retaliation.

JURY DUTY

Under some state laws, including California law, employers are not allowed to fire or discriminate against an employee called to serve as a juror or testify as a witness, provided the employee gives reasonable advance notice for time off. That said, employers are typically not required to pay wages while an employee serves as a juror or witness. Therefore, your policy in this area may want to state whether and for how long wages and benefits are provided during jury leave.

FAMILY AND MEDICAL LEAVE

Under federal law, employers with 50 or more employees (fewer in some states) must provide eligible employees unpaid family and medical care leave of up to three months in a 12-month period. Leaves can be taken to care for a newborn or adopted child, or a child, spouse or parent with a serious health condition. In addition, employees unable to work due to pregnancy-related conditions may take up to four months of disability leave, in addition to their maternity leave.

Maternity and medical leaves are typically granted under the expectation that an employee will be eligible to return to work. And the law prohibits discrimination on the basis of pregnancy, childbirth or related medical conditions. Therefore, your policy in this area should be carefully crafted and clearly specify the circumstances under which maternity and medical leaves will be granted. It should also outline the employee's obligations while on leave.

To learn more about developing a personnel policy, consult a reputable guide such as the *Employee Handbook and Personnel Policies Manual* by Richard J. Simmons, LLP, L.A.

KEEP IT CURRENT!

▶ Employment laws change regularly, and your policies should too. Review often and update policies entirely every three years to ensure they are correct under the law.

A nonprofit's personnel policy is no different from any other employer. It should include information on benefits, employee conduct, grievance procedures or concerns and disclosure of an employee's legal rights.

QUICK TIP

Q | How do we determine compensation and benefits packages?

A Your organization's approach to compensation will affect your ability to attract, retain and motivate qualified and enthusiastic employees. So how do you determine how to set appropriate yet attractive salaries and give increases and benefits? Here are some ideas to get you started:

SET SALARIES THAT FIT.

In Southern California, the Center for Nonprofit Management (CNM) publishes an annual compensation and benefits survey for nonprofit employers located in Southern and Central California. To purchase a copy, visit the CNM website (www.cnmsocal.org/salarysurvey).

Next, you'll want to look at your organization in relation to others in your service area. Check competitors and partner associations. Look at individual roles in your organization and compare market pay scales for each position.

Search job sites for job titles that match, and look for salary information. Reach out to professional associations for salary studies or trend reports. Or, try one of the many salary calculators available online.

Then, look at how positions fit within your organization. Determine value based on the skills and experience necessary to perform the job, as well as output and how integral the position is to your organization's success.

To help ensure fair decision-making when evaluating and compensating potential and current employees, establish a salary range for each position. You'll want a minimum and a maximum salary, with the midpoint being your target for fully effective performance.

CONSIDER OFFERING OTHER BENEFITS, PARTICULARLY WHEN BUDGETS ARE TIGHT.

It's well known that salaries in the nonprofit sector are lower than those in the corporate sector. And nonprofit job seekers often choose the work for reasons that go beyond compensation. This makes benefit packages a big factor in recruiting and retaining nonprofit employees.

HOW TO DETERMINE A SALARY RANGE?

▸ Try dividing the salary minimum by a factor and then adding the result to the minimum. For example, a 50 percent salary range based on a minimum of $24,000 can be calculated by dividing by 2 ($12,000) and adding that to the minimum ($24,000 + $12,000 = $36,000). Here, $24,000 is the minimum, $30,000 is the midpoint and $36,000 is the maximum.

Since employers are not required to provide benefits, plans will vary widely depending on an organization's size, field of service and budget constraints. If offered, benefits can include paid vacation; holidays; sick time; training opportunities; health, dental, life, and disability insurance; and retirement benefits. In addition, you may want to build in other attractive benefits, such as flexible working hours or the ability to work from home, gym memberships or even an office lunch program.

If you do decide to offer benefits, you must abide by state and federal laws that regulate them. Therefore, you'll want to clearly define who is eligible for benefits and when, the types and amounts of benefits available, and the circumstances under which benefits may be lost or forfeited. Also be sure to document your right to modify or terminate benefit features as needed.

SET GUIDELINES FOR COMPENSATION INCREASES.

When do increases happen? Will increases be available for promotion or transfer? Tie consideration for salary increases to performance and set regular performance reviews and you set fair standards for all.

❝ Do your job and demand your compensation — but in that order. ❞

- Cary Grant, Actor

Check out the Center for Nonprofit Management's compensation and benefits survey (www.cnmsocal.org/salarysurvey) to better understand trends in nonprofit employment.

QUICK TIP

NO.
6

Q How do we evaluate staff and executive director performance?

A Performance evaluations are key to keeping communication lines open, effectively managing people and getting their best, everyday. Evaluations encourage individuals to achieve goals, and correct performance issues. They help employers provide employees with necessary support and may protect employers from false claims of wrongful termination. And, the review is also an opportunity to update job descriptions.

Employee evaluations are generally conducted by an immediate supervisor. For the executive director, a board member should lead the effort.

Following are some key factors to consider:

DEVELOP A REGULAR SCHEDULE FOR EVALUATIONS.

Depending on your needs, consider conducting employee evaluations annually, semi-annually or quarterly. They should be conducted on the same date for all employees or on the anniversary of an employee's hire. Also remember to give ongoing feedback to boost morale and correct issues in real-time.

BE CLEAR AND OBJECTIVE ABOUT PERFORMANCE STANDARDS.

Develop a standard evaluation form for use organization-wide, to ensure balanced, fair results.

Keep the discussion positive, but don't be afraid to accurately reflect performance. Discuss both strengths and weaknesses using specific examples where expectations have been met, exceeded or fallen short. If performance is low, set a date to review progress.

Once the form has been discussed with the employee, be sure it is understood. Leave space for employee comments and a signature.

BOARD EVALUATIONS OF THE EXECUTIVE DIRECTOR SHOULD NOT BE MISSED.

Executive director evaluations are a significant component of a board's responsibilities. They are critical to ensuring an executive director is in sync with a board, and driving the organization toward its mission. Evaluations also help to clarify expectations and goals.

As with employees, it's important to establish clear, consistent criteria and processes for executive director evaluations. You'll also want to set regular reviews, at least annually.

QUESTIONS TO CONSIDER BEFORE EVALUATING AN EXECUTIVE DIRECTOR:

▶ Who will be involved in the evaluation?

▶ What form will the evaluation take – 360°, feedback, meeting of performance goals, or …?

▶ How will future goals be established?

▶ How is the evaluation and review tied to compensation?

Q } What precautions should a nonprofit take when disciplining or firing an employee?

A } Taking disciplinary action or terminating an employee is never easy. It affects organizational morale, taps resources and, if not handled properly, could result in lawsuits.

To minimize risk, develop clear guidelines for performance reviews. Truthfully document employee progress, and track disciplinary measures as they happen.

If you do need to let an employee go, termination should be based on:

- An employee not adequately performing specific job duties.

- An employee violating a written organizational policy, such as harassing another employee.

Generally, a court will uphold an employer's right to fire an employee as long as the termination does not violate discrimination laws, protective statutes or the employer's contractual commitments.

HERE'S AN EXAMPLE. Your employee handbook states an employee will not be disciplined or fired without cause. You have also developed a grievance policy to help resolve disputes. In this case, a court would be more likely to uphold a "wrongful discharge" claim from an employee who is fired for supposed harassment but was denied the opportunity to use the grievance procedure to try to resolve the issue.

If you do develop written policy that outlines the kind of performance that would result in disciplinary action or termination, be sure to describe the types of offenses carefully. And don't forget to include a statement that indicates that examples cited are intended as illustration only. Finally, it's essential that you engage legal counsel to review all human resources policies.

▶ When disciplining or terminating an employee, documentation is critical. A disciplined employee should receive and sign a "write-up," which is then placed in the employee file. Leading up to termination, an employer should document all actions (time, date, circumstances) that factor into the termination decision.

No. **8**

Q ⟩ How do we choose and vet a consultant?

A ⟩ You need an outside perspective and you want to hire a consultant. You're looking for someone with the expertise and objectivity to help you move forward and succeed. Where do you start?

FIRST DETERMINE YOUR NEEDS.

Begin by examining your own organizational goals to determine what it is you really need help with. This is best achieved by determining your objectives and outlining any strategies you've applied to meet them.

Think about your resources. How much time do your employees and volunteers have available to dedicate to the tasks necessary to reach your goals? Do they have the requisite skills to achieve the right results? Answering these questions will enable you to identify gaps and define the tasks a consultant may take on. This will help you make the best use of any consultant you hire.

WHEN YOU'RE READY TO HIRE, DEVELOP CRITERIA TO EVALUATE CANDIDATES.

Develop a list of questions to help you select candidates that fit. Interview at least two to three consultants before making a decision and be sure to discuss:

- Experience in your area of need and with your type of organization.

- Interest in the work your organization does.

- Track records of success.

- Their approach to working with nonprofits – show they plan to structure and check in on the work, and how they define expected outcomes.

- Cost estimates, what fees include, and how payment will be structured.

▶ If you're going to engage consultants regularly, use an attorney to develop a standard consultant contract. This will ensure that legal and insurance needs are met, while outlining the expectations and duties of consultants.

Before you engage a consultant, be sure you understand the legal difference between a "consultant" and an "employee."

QUICK TIP

- Time frames for completion, and other commitments that might limit available time.

- Expectations for support from your employees, how you work and the resources you have available.

Once you've found a match, consider vetting your selection with professional colleagues. Before work commences, ask the consultant to sign your standard non-disclosure agreement and develop a contract with the consultant so terms and expectations are clear. Ask the consultant to provide work plans, contract amounts, billing arrangements, reporting structure and termination procedures.

For more information about working with consultants, refer to a reputable guide such as Nonprofit Consultants: How To Choose Them, How To Use Them. Find it at www.first5la.org (click on Resources/ Consultant Resource Directory). Another resource is the National Network of Consultants to Grantmakers directory - http://www.nncg. org/directory/search/.

If you need to take a step back from day-to-day operations and plot out the long-term direction of your user experience strategy, consultants can give you a perspective you can't get on your own.

- Jesse James Garrett, CEO, Adaptive Path

Visit www.nonprofitanswerguide.org for timely sector resources and more expert answers to your most immediate nonprofit questions.

QUICK TIP

No. **9**

Q Are we ready to work with volunteers?

A As your nonprofit grows, you'll have a need to get more people involved to meet your objectives. While bringing on a volunteer or two doesn't require too much organization, if you're considering developing a more sophisticated volunteer program, you'll want to assess your readiness to take on the task.

Here are three key questions to address before jumping into volunteer program development:

1. DO YOU HAVE SOMEONE TO RECRUIT, SELECT AND SUPERVISE MULTIPLE VOLUNTEERS? Volunteers are best evaluated, trained and managed by one representative within the organization. And the task of bringing on and managing volunteers requires planning and dedicated time.

2. HAVE YOU GARNERED STAFF AND MANAGEMENT SUPPORT FOR YOUR VOLUNTEER PROGRAM? Getting the entire organization on-board and involved in creating an appropriate program is a key to success. Tap staff and management to develop a plan. Have them help establish goals for involving volunteers, to make sure goals are consistent with staff roles. Volunteers should be brought on to support staff positions, not infringe on them.

3. DO YOU HAVE AN ORIENTATION PLAN? Before you recruit volunteers, you're going to want to develop formal procedures to help you orient volunteers to the organization and train them for specific job functions.

▶ Don't forget to consider whether or not you need insurance to cover your volunteers' activities. This can include their use of autos or equipment, as well as the organization's liability.

❝ It is amazing how much people get done if they do not worry about who gets the credit. ❞

- Swahili proverb

Q How can we create a successful volunteer program?

A Volunteers can be terrific champions for your organization. And starting a volunteer program can be an exciting process. But often these programs grow haphazardly out of an immediate need to bring in additional resources. When this happens, problems can arise. Communication between staff and volunteers can break down, contributions to the organization's mission may be missed, and volunteer retention may become a challenge.

Before you begin, create a solid foundation. People volunteer because they care about an issue, want to be around others who are of like mind, and want to do meaningful work. Keep this in mind as you develop your volunteer program. Plan thoroughly and you'll have a better chance of success.

DEVELOP A PLAN AND GET BUY-IN FROM STAFF AND MANAGEMENT.

Identify a need for your program. Define program goals that connect to organizational values, and develop a policy around volunteer involvement. Make sure to involve staff in planning and get full support from management to set your program up for success. Getting everyone to contribute will help you develop a strong model that clearly details how volunteers can take on needed tasks and support staff positions without slowing down overall productivity.

▶ Remember the essentials for good volunteer management: recruitment, orientation, coordination and retention.

TREAT VOLUNTEER RECRUITMENT SERIOUSLY.

Create engaging recruitment messages to encourage volunteer participation. Develop thoughtful volunteer job descriptions to further identify needs and ensure expectations are clear. Be creative about where you look for volunteers. Reach out to friends and colleagues, partner associations and board members for referrals. And before you select a candidate, carefully evaluate each potential volunteer just as you would an employee.

Volunteers are the lifeblood of many nonprofit organizations. A sound volunteer recruitment and management plan will ensure that you, and they, are able to gain maximum benefit from the experience.

QUICK TIP

No. 10

BE READY FOR ORIENTATION AND TRAINING.

Plan in advance how you'll orient volunteers about the organization and train them for specific job functions. Train staff on how to communicate with volunteers and explain the chain of command. Proper training and orientation will clarify expectations and help your volunteers prepare to dive in.

COORDINATE VOLUNTEER INVOLVEMENT AND MONITOR PROGRESS.

You'll want to designate a single individual to manage volunteers, track their progress, and monitor interaction between staff, volunteers and constituents. Having volunteers report to a single individual helps keep communication lines open and reduces the likelihood that expectations are not met.

If problems arise, be ready to adjust. Document your progress to help you do so.

ENCOURAGE PARTICIPATION AND ADJUST STRATEGIES AS NEEDED TO RETAIN GOOD VOLUNTEERS.

Provide regular feedback and program results to staff and volunteers to boost morale and encourage new ideas for volunteer involvement. And remember, recognition is key to retaining volunteers. Volunteer retention saves time and effort and allows you to focus on program goals over recruiting. So look for low-cost ways to thank volunteers for a job well done.

One man can be a crucial ingredient on a team, but one man cannot make a team.
- Kareem Abdul-Jabbar

Looking for volunteers in Southern California? Try www.vcla.net in the Los Angeles area, and www.volunteercenter.org in Orange County.

QUICK TIP

HR MANAGEMENT

- *First, Break All the Rules,* by Marcus Buckingham and Curt Coffman

- **Free Management Library: All About Human Resources and Talent Management** (www.managementhelp.org/humanresources/index.htm)

- **Workforce Management** (www.workforce.com)

BUSINESS LEADERSHIP

- **The CBS Interactive Business Network** (www.bnet.com)

READY-TO-GO-RESOURCES

20-SECOND-SUMMARY

- Before you hire, know what you're looking for. Remember, a job description is an advertisement not only for the position, but also for your organization.

- Remember, you're bound by your policies, so make sure they're not more restrictive than legally necessary.

- Be sure that you're using independent contractors correctly. Misclassifying an employee as an independent contractor can get you into trouble and result in IRS penalties.

- Be clear and positive about performance evaluation standards. Set goals and keep discussions present and future-oriented, rather than just discussing the past.

- Vet potential consultants thoroughly. Once you've found a match, develop contracts before work commences.

- Volunteers can be an added value to your organization. However, they must be managed and given job descriptions and clear tasks to perform effectively.

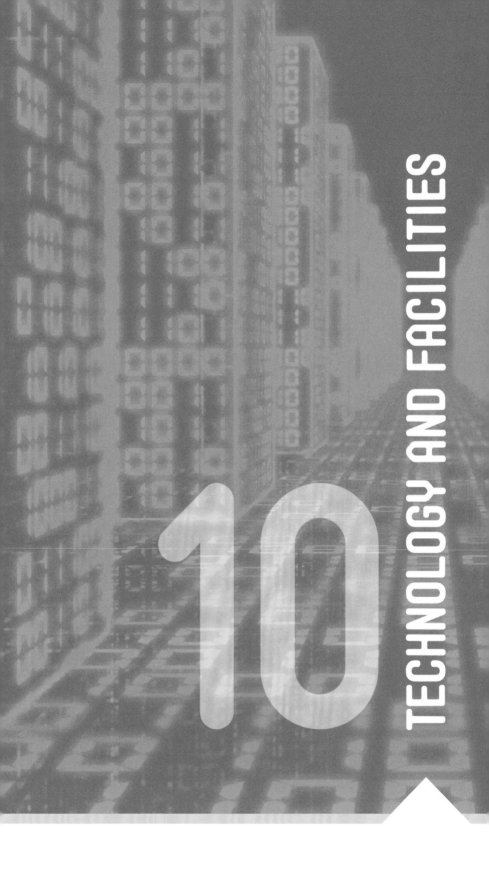

10

TECHNOLOGY AND FACILITIES

Technology is about a lot more than having a million people "like" your Facebook page.

A sound technology infrastructure can boost your organization's effectiveness, help you connect with key stakeholders, increase awareness and raise funds. The challenge for nonprofits is that technology usually requires an upfront investment, but it can payoff in spades.

Here, we cover the basics around when and how to adopt new technology, leveraging technology to support marketing, turning social media into social good, and whether/how to hire a consultant. We also offer up some resources on how to get technology funded. And, since the backbone of technology is infrastructure, we've included some advice on issues related to facilities, such as finding shared office space and the impact of the Americans with Disabilities Act.

And the best news? There are a lot of low-cost and no-cost resources out there. This chapter gives you a rundown of some of our favorites.

Q | When is a nonprofit ready to adopt technology?

A In a sector where financial support is typically directed to programming activities over innovation, nonprofits tend to lag behind their corporate counterparts when it comes to utilizing new technologies. As a result, they often remain tech-shy.

That said, there should be a place for technology in every nonprofit, regardless of type, size, operational budget or life stage. With limited time, resources and funding, the key is learning how to make technology work for your organization today, keeping an eye to the future.

Unsure how to take the first step? Think about how you can use technology to improve productivity and reduce costs, automate repetitive or time-consuming tasks, organize information and engage your constituents.

You'll also want to do your research to ensure you're choosing technology that meets not only your budget but also your needs. To help make sense of the multitude of hardware, software, applications and networking options available, consider recruiting a professional to conduct a technology evaluation and help you understand how you can align your organizational goals with available technology.

YOU'RE READY WHEN:

▶ Daily activities take too much time, or may be repetitive and could be automated.

▶ You have too much information stored in paper files, or information is difficult to retrieve and disseminate.

▶ You want to enhance productivity, collaboration and communication; better serve your constituents; and help your organization run smoothly.

Invest now and start taking advantage of the benefits technology has to offer.

QUICK TIP

No. **2**

Q How can nonprofit executives use technology to maximize their effectiveness?

A Technology is essential to your organization's success. But how do you leverage it on a budget, for maximum results with minimal disruption to your operations?

HERE'S HOW TO MAKE TECHNOLOGY WORK FOR YOU AND YOUR ORGANIZATION:

Put your organizational goals first. Then, consider how you can integrate technology to help you reach your objectives. Weigh costs and benefits and use technology only where it makes sense for your organization.

▶ For all of the expensive technology out there, there is just as much inexpensive (or free!) technology. Get familiar with available tools to increase efficiency and exposure.

Treat technology investments like any other operational expense. Create a budget for your technology needs. Plan for maintenance and upgrades and you won't be surprised by unexpected expenses.

Investigate time- and cost-saving technology tools — such as wireless networks, instant messenger, online meeting tools and workspaces, constituent relationship management tools and more — to improve productivity and stretch limited resources. Look for compatible technologies that easily integrate together.

Consider adopting a virtual working environment. Taking on in-house employees can be cost-prohibitive for budget-conscious nonprofits. Virtual working environments allow remote workers and contractors to easily connect to the office regardless of time or geographical location.

Use affordable online marketing strategies as a way to balance the expense of traditional marketing. Build a website and use social media to maximize exposure and grow awareness about your mission.

Technology eases the burden of tracking constituents, donations and more. Investigate low-cost management tools such as Salesforce, Infusionsoft, intouchcrm, Click & Pledge, PayPal Donations, Google Checkout and the like. Visit idealware.org for recommendations.

Know what you want to achieve with your mission and let technology follow.

QUICK TIP

Q | Where can we integrate technology into our nonprofit and what kinds of tools are available?

A Used smartly, technology can help you do more with less. But in a fast-changing industry, how do you keep pace with what's available? And just as importantly, how do you determine where to put your dollars and resources? The Internet is a good place to begin your research. Technology information and review sites such as idealware.org and NTEN provide articles and product comparison reports, and offer recommendations targeted to the unique needs of nonprofits.

To start, consider putting technology to use in the following areas:

OFFICE INFRASTRUCTURE

A sound office framework is critical to the success of your organization. As such, integrating technology into your office operations should be your first priority. When budgeting for technology outputs in this area, computer hardware and software, databases, networking and security should be taken into account. The complexity of technical options may seem overwhelming, so consider hiring an IT consultant to help you choose tools that effectively meet your needs and budget, and account for future growth.

FUNDRAISING

Fundraising in the nonprofit sector is undergoing a technology revolution. Thanks to the growth of open source technologies, a plethora of innovative donation and outreach tools, and the rise of social media sites like Facebook and Twitter, nonprofits can quickly and cost effectively implement grassroots campaigns using leading technology tools.

Many nonprofits are also integrating mobile giving into their fundraising strategies. Check out Chapter 5: Fundraising, to learn more about how to set up a mobile giving system and find resources that are available to assist you.

EVENT MANAGEMENT

No matter what type of nonprofit you are, your constituency is going to want to register for events online. Fortunately, there are a wide variety of tools available to help you accept and manage registration and payment for seminars, courses, conferences and other events. From basic and affordable, to feature-rich integrated systems, you're

▶ Technology touches every aspect of your nonprofit. Up-to-date hardware and software are likely to be the backbone of your operations. After that, your online, mobile and networked presence will have an enormous influence on core area areas including marketing, communications and development.

sure to find a tool that meets your needs and budget. Take a look at PayPal®, Acteva, Constant Contact® and Cvent to start.

MEMBER AND CONSTITUENT MANAGEMENT

Constituent relationship management (CRM) applications help organizations manage the many different relationships they may have with constituents, members, volunteers, donors, partners and more. For nonprofits, CRM is available ready to use as an online system, can be purchased as a software package and installed on office computers, or can even be cost effectively customized using an open source option. The Raiser's Edge and Blackbaud Enterprise are CRM solutions you've likely already heard of. However, there are many options out there, each with their own pros and cons, so you'll want to spend time researching the right solution for your needs.

COLLABORATION AND COMMUNICATION

Technology makes communication and collaboration easy, keeps projects on track, and helps remote workers stay connected to the office.

You probably already use email, but instant messaging (IM) tools such as Skype, AIM and Google Talk are also efficient ways to communicate, person to person or in groups. IM is faster than email and ideal for quick exchanges, to determine who's available or to get immediate feedback.

For project collaboration tasks, look at online project management tools such as Basecamp and Yammer. These project-specific workspaces allow you and your colleagues to organize, exchange and update information from office, home or anywhere work takes you.

Also consider wikis and FTP sites to give and gain access to large files and keep collaborative files current.

Looking for an alternative to in-person meetings? Try web or video conferencing tools such as Adobe Connect, GoToMeeting, Microsoft Office Live Meeting and the like. Today's sophisticated meeting tools effectively gather remote users together to meet online in real time by offering features such as video, audio and text chat, screen and document sharing, slide presentations and more.

Wondering about that "cloud" everyone seems to be talking about? The cloud is comprised of applications, services and data that exist somewhere other than on your computer. In other words, all of the tools we've described above exist in the cloud.

MARKETING AND PR

Without exception, technology should be part of every nonprofit organization's marketing mix.

At minimum, your nonprofit should have a website. Keep design and language simple, build "'search-engine friendly" to your constituent needs, and you can't go wrong. You may also want to hire a search engine optimization (SEO) specialist to optimize your site to rank well in search engines like Google and Yahoo. An SEO specialist will use techniques, such as researching and incorporating select keywords and phrases into your website, to help boost your position online and attract targeted visitors.

And keep in mind site maintenance. Ideally, you'll want to update your own website. A good content management system (CMS) can help you do that. Take a look at cost-effective open source systems such as WordPress and Drupal to start.

To send professional and appealing e-newsletters, alerts and fundraising requests, try broadcast email tools such as Constant Contact®, MailChimp and VerticalResponse®. Or, quickly survey your constituents online with tools like SurveyMonkey™.

Consider advertising online. Even if your resources are limited, you have options here. For example, Google Grants offers in-kind AdWords advertising to select charitable organizations. To learn more, visit www.google.com/grants.

When you're ready, join the conversation! Listen to your constituents and build relationships online using social media tools like Facebook, LinkedIn and Twitter. You can also manage your brand with web-monitoring tools such as Google Alerts and Technorati, and distribute press releases through services such as PRWeb™.

If you have the right human resources and a steady stream of fresh content, you might also consider blogging as a way to promote your message and inform stakeholders. A blog can be hosted on your own website, or you can use free services available at blogger.com or wordpress.com. If you decide to go this route, just remember to cross-promote your posts on your social networks.

Visit www.nonprofitanswerguide.org **for timely sector resources and more expert answers to your most immediate nonprofit questions.**

QUICK TIP

NO.

4

Q | How can a nonprofit successfully manage its technology? How can a consultant help?

A | Running a successful nonprofit requires a clear focus on your mission and organizational goals. The same is true when it comes to managing technology. Keep an eye on objectives, set goals for technology, and evaluate costs versus benefits for any technology you're considering. In short, develop a plan. This is best achieved when technology tools and strategies, budget outlays, and evaluation systems are integrated directly into your operational plan.

At every stage of operations, consider how you can use technology to reduce time and costs and improve productivity, now and in the future. Think about your ability to support and maintain the tools and strategies you choose. Then, implement only those you can handle. It's possible to do more damage than good when you adopt technology that you don't have the resources or dollars to support.

Think about what you can implement and manage in-house and what may require the help of a professional. If you have the budget, consider hiring a technology consultant to assist with short- and long-term planning, implement new technologies and solve problems.

A variety of technology consultants are available for hire. Strategic advisors can help when you don't have the time or resources to research options yourself. They will communicate trends, recommend solutions to meet your particular needs and help you plan for the future. A computer support or network consultant will engage in tactical work, helping to implement and maintain technology and troubleshoot issues. Design and marketing consultants can help you develop an online presence and promote your cause via email, events, social media and the like. Recruiting an expert in any of these areas will help you avoid costly mistakes and manage growth.

WHERE TO LOOK FOR TECHNICAL CONSULTANTS SERVING NONPROFITS:

▶ TechSoup
(www.techsoup.org)

▶ NPower
(www.npower.org)

▶ netCorps
(www.netcorps.org)

▶ Idealist
(www.idealist.org)

Starting with clear operational objectives and recognizing when technology can't solve your problem is half the battle.

QUICK TIP

Q | How can technology be funded?

A | In the nonprofit sector, where funding is typically targeted toward mission-based activities, finding the dollars to invest in your technology infrastructure can be a challenge. But the task is not insurmountable.

With a little research, you'll find a number of organizations dedicated to connecting nonprofits with technology. Many are targeted to facilitating donations or connecting organizations with professionals offering low-cost or pro bono technology-related services. Tapping into the technology skills and expertise of volunteers can be an effective way to stretch a limited budget.

Adding technology to all grant requests will increase your chances of success. When looking for funding from foundations or individual donors, build technology expenses into your programming budgets and thoroughly explain how technology will support or expand each program. According to Sue Bennett, "The Accidental Techie," funders want to see that the implementation of technology is solidly aligned with an organization's mission.

And don't overlook corporate sponsors and partners. Corporations – especially those in the technology industry – can be a valuable resource for technology funding or to provide in-kind donations in exchange for advertising at events, on your website and the like. Hardware donations from technology companies can be of great value to nonprofits. However, if you're considering accepting used donations from individuals, you'll want to give careful consideration to whether the benefits outweigh the costs. Organizations that accept used technology run the risk of receiving outdated hardware that takes time and effort to get up and running. In the end, it may take more work on your part than it's worth.

GET STARTED HERE:

▸ Visit TechMD (www.techmd.com) for a vetted list of private, corporate and public funders that support technology for nonprofits.

▸ Connect with NPower (www.npower.org), a network that brings IT services to nonprofits.

▸ Join TechSoup (www.techsoup.org) and access technology donations for nonprofits.

Don't give up! Remember, technology is an investment in your organization's future.

QUICK TIP

No.
6

Q › Can we design our own website? What are the key factors to keep in mind?

A › Choosing between designing and building a website yourself or hiring a professional to do the job for you is often simply a matter of what you can afford and have the capacity for. Fortunately, for budget-conscious nonprofits, there are cost-effective options that allow you to design and build your own website with little or no coding knowledge.

Popular tools such as WordPress and Intuit offer website templates that allow you to pick a design and add your own graphics and text through intuitive interfaces made for users with little technical experience. These tools are typically low-cost, purchased for a one-time fee, or "rented" on a monthly basis. Some are even free.

Do-it-yourself web building tools are an ideal choice for shoestring nonprofits without a need for complex site features such as robust search functions, e-commerce or interactivity.

That said, if you are tech savvy or have the budget to hire a professional, starting with a website template and modifying it to suit more complex needs can also be a cost-effective alternative to designing and building a website from scratch.

If you don't have a web designer on staff, but want to design and build a custom website from the ground up, you'll definitely want to seek professional assistance. A good web designer will help you plan, create and launch an accessible, attractive and easily maintained site that hits the mark.

BEFORE YOU START, HERE ARE SEVEN KEY FACTORS TO KEEP IN MIND:

1. **DEVELOP A PLAN.** Determine your website objectives. Define your users and build to their needs. Start by researching your market online. Visit competitor websites. What are they doing that you like; what could they do better? Draw inspiration there.

2. **THINK ABOUT SITE ARCHITECTURE.** How many pages do you need and how will they be structured? Map your content to each page and, if content runs long, consider adding subpages to create visual breaks. Develop five scenarios of who might come to your

site and what they might want to do. This will help you develop site architecture based on what your visitors will be looking for. It'll also help ensure you've considered all of your audiences.

3. **WHEN IN DOUBT, CHOOSE SIMPLICITY OVER BELLS AND WHISTLES.** Busy sites can confuse users or even turn them away. A good website is clean and functional. It's easy to navigate, consistently organized and succinctly written in plain language.

4. **MAINTAINING YOUR SITE IS AS IMPORTANT AS BUILDING IT.** Before you build, consider a content management system (CMS). A CMS is the back-end of your website that site visitors don't see. It'll allow you to maintain your site without professional intervention. Web builder tools typically offer a user-friendly CMS built right into the product.

5. **BUILD YOUR SITE SEARCH-ENGINE FRIENDLY.** If you're choosing a do-it-yourself tool, ensure the product you choose allows you to optimize your site for search engines. Be careful of sites that feature too much Flash, as these can inhibit your chances of being found in engines like Google.

6. **BUILD YOUR SITE TO BE DONATION-FRIENDLY.** Nonprofits usually rely on donations, so it's essential that your site makes it as easy as possible for a donor to give. This means highlighting your "donate now" option on your homepage. For more information, check out Chapter 5: Fundraising.

7. **TEST YOUR SITE BEFORE YOU LAUNCH.** Recruit staff, clients or colleagues to review your site for functionality and errors. Remember, your website is your face to the world and often the first place people will turn to learn about you.

HIRING A PROFESSIONAL?

▸ Shop around before you buy.

▸ Industry rates vary widely and you don't always get what you pay for. Do your research and get more than one quote before hiring anyone to help you.

Visit WordPress to see examples of websites that have been built using templates as a foundation (www.wordpress.org/showcase).

QUICK TIP

NO. **7**

Q | What is social media?

A You've probably already used a social media tool or two for business or personal purposes. Examples include consumer review websites, email and instant messaging, blogs, forums and message boards, wikis, podcasts, photo and video sharing technologies, web-based project collaboration tools and more.

Simply put, social media is an umbrella term used to describe the myriad of web-based and mobile technologies that facilitate social interaction and the sharing of words, photos and video.

As opposed to traditional media (TV, newspapers, print and the like) which pushes information out to an audience, social media relies on audience participation as a driver, allowing individuals with common interests to quickly and easily use technology to interact and exchange information in the electronic world. The goal of the social media phenomenon is to encourage free dialogue by making information exchange a democratic process.

For marketing purposes, think of social media as a toolkit that can help you tap into the growing trend toward peer-to-peer recommendations and referrals. Social media can be an inexpensive way to listen to your constituents, build relationships, establish credibility, promote your mission, and grow trust about you and your organization.

For more information on social media tools and the role it can play in advancing your objectives, see Chapter 6: Marketing and Communications.

▸ Facebook and Twitter are probably the most well-known social media tools available. Twitter lets you send short messages out across the Internet to users who choose to "follow" you, while Facebook lets you interact with others in a more complex communications environment. Other popular examples include LinkedIn, YouTube and Flickr.

There's a communication revolution going on. It's instantaneous, multi-directional and it often happens among strangers who will never meet face to face.

QUICK TIP

Q } How can nonprofits use social media for social good?

A } You know what social media is, and maybe you've even experimented with tools like Facebook and LinkedIn. But you're still unsure how to tap into the power of social media to make it work for your mission. Where do you turn? Fortunately, there's a growing trend among experts toward learning how to use social media effectively to meet the unique needs of the nonprofit sector.

Psychology, marketing and entrepreneurship experts, Jennifer Aaker and Andy Smith, for example, have developed a framework to help nonprofits use social media to create positive impact. They call the result the Dragonfly Effect, symbolizing the integration of four "wings" synchronized to take flight. These "wings" represent a series of steps an organization can take to get results, and are a simple way to think about developing a social media campaign.

HOW TO CREATE THE DRAGONFLY EFFECT:

WING 1: **FOCUS.** Identify a single goal you want to achieve with your social media campaign and use it as your driving force. Make it realistic and measurable. Create an action plan around your goal.

WING 2: **GRAB ATTENTION.** Develop a "hook." Make it original, memorable and authentic. Consider using visual imagery.

WING 3: **ENGAGE.** Tell a story and make it personal. Connect to your audience's emotions.

WING 4: **TAKE ACTION.** Get your audience moving for your cause. Ask for time, donations or both and make it easy for your audience to contribute.

Social media offers a ton of opportunities to connect with your audience and advance your organization. However, it's important to remember that social media represents a platform for your organization's voice. It can be a very high-profile communications vehicle (sometimes unintentionally so), so it's essential that you carefully select the staff charged with running your social media effort. It's tempting to simply assign it to an intern since young people are often savvy about new technology, but that can also be very risky.

▶ Read more about the Dragonfly Effect in the *Stanford Social Innovation Review*, Winter 2011 issue.

No. 8

Another important area to consider is the ability to serve as a resource and thought leader on your issue through social media. It's not simply a venue to tell people what you're doing (although that's important too). Instead, think about how you can use social media to engage people in a conversation about the broader issues of importance to your field and community. This keeps people involved and informed, and helps to position you as an expert.

The use of social platforms to encourage cause-related change simply makes sense for nonprofits with limited budgets and resources. With a little planning and a lot of enthusiasm, you can make it work for you.

▶ Constant engagement is an important component of a successful social media effort. Figure out what your organization has to offer that can add value to your target audiences' lives. Personal stories, objective research, aggregation of news from the field, evaluation results... all of these can provide fodder for your social media presence.

How can you squander even one more day not taking advantage of the greatest shifts of our generation? How dare you settle for less when the world has made it so easy for you to be remarkable?

- Seth Godin, Author

Armed with a cause, a plan and a few good online tools, it's possible to change the world.

QUICK TIP

Q } How can an organization find low cost or shared office space?

A } For nonprofits on a budget, finding a place to call home can be a challenge. But you have more options than you think.

Start by reaching out to nonprofit networks for direction. Many networks across the country support incubator-style work centers where nonprofits gather to share resources and ideas. The NonprofitCenters Network (www.nonprofitcenters.org), for example, is dedicated to supporting the development of multi-tenant nonprofit centers. To further this mission, they offer a searchable database advertising multi-tenant workspaces designed specifically to support nonprofit needs.

Virtual office services or executive co-working centers can also be a cost-effective alternative for nonprofits that may not need day-to-day operational space. Many virtual services offer telephone answering services, mailboxes and shared equipment, in addition to office spaces and meeting rooms that can be rented by the hour, the day, the month, or year to year.

You might also consider making an arrangement with a building owner for free or discounted space. Tap board members, volunteers and donors to find owners who may want to boost occupancy. And be sure to visit the Southern California Association of NonProfit Housing (www.scanph.org) for shared or low-cost office space listings.

More and more nonprofits are sharing space to maximize resources. Search for opportunities the same way you would search for your own space – through leasing agents, colleagues in your field and online postings.

QUICK TIP

NO.

10

▶ If you have employees, clients or a facility, there's a good chance you'll need to be compliant with certain provisions of the Americans with Disabilities Act. Check out www.ada.gov to learn more about the provisions that apply to your organization.

Q What is the Americans with Disabilities Act? How does it affect our office space?

A The Americans with Disabilities Act ensures equal opportunity for persons with disabilities in employment, state and local government services, public accommodations, commercial facilities, transportation and telecommunications.

As a building owner or a tenant, this includes making reasonable accommodations to office spaces to ensure they're accessible for use by all. Examples include providing ramps, widening doorways, reconfiguring shelves, moving toilet stall partitions to accommodate wheelchairs and installing grab bars.

Under this Act, disability accommodations should be "reasonably achievable" and not cause financial hardship to the owner or tenant.

To learn more about the Act, visit the ADA website at www.ada.gov.

❝ The moral test of government is how it treats those who are in the dawn of life... the children; those who are in the twilight of life...the elderly; and those who are in the shadow of life...the sick...the needy... and the disabled. ❞

- Hubert H. Humphrey

GENERAL ADVICE AND INFORMATION

- **Idealware**
  (www.idealware.org)
- **NTEN**
  (www.nten.org)
- **TechSoup**
  (www.techsoup.org)

ASSISTANCE PROVIDERS

- **NPower**
  (www.npower.org)
- **Progressive Technology Project**
  (www.progressivetech.org)
- **Taproot Foundation**
  (www.taprootfoundation.org)

FUNDRAISING AND SOCIAL MEDIA

- **The Networked Nonprofit,**
  by Beth Kanter and Allison Fine
- **Network for Good**
  (www.fundraising123.org)

BLOGS

- **Beth Kanter's Blog**
  (www.bethkanter.org)
- **Michelle Murrain's Blog**
  (www.zenofnptech.org)

TECH PROGRAMS FOR NONPROFITS

- **Google for Nonprofits Program**
  (google.com/nonprofits)
- **Youtube Good Work Program**
  (www.youtube.com/goodwork)

READY-TO-GO-RESOURCES

20-SECOND-SUMMARY

- Treat technology investments like any other operational expense and write them into your budget. And don't forget to plan for maintenance and upgrades.

- Don't let technology drive you. First, decide what you want to achieve. Then, weigh the costs and benefits of adopting anything new.

- Develop a website that delivers. Your website is your face to the world and often the first place people will go to learn about you. Keep it clean and easy to navigate.

- Use low-cost online marketing techniques to balance traditional marketing. Think email marketing, search engine optimization, social media and the like.

- If you don't know the answer, ask a professional! Tapping into expert knowledge can save you time and help you avoid costly mistakes.

- Industry rates vary widely, so always get more than one quote. That way, you'll be sure you're paying a fair price for the services you procure.

REFERENCES

CHAPTER 1: LEADERSHIP

Bell, J., Masaoka, J., & Zimmerman, S. (2010). *Nonprofit Sustainability: Making Strategic Decisions for Financial Viability.* San Francisco, CA: Jossey-Bass.

Chait, R.P., Holland, T. & Taylor, B. (September-October 1996). **The New Work of the Nonprofit Board.** *Harvard Business Review.* Retrieved July 25, 2011, from http://www.hbr.org/1996/09/the-new-work-of-the-nonprofit-board/ar/1.

Connolly, P. & Lukas, C. (2002). *Strengthening Nonprofit Performance: A Funder's Guide to Capacity Building.* St. Paul: Amherst H. Wilder Foundation.

Crutchfield, L. & McLeod Grant, H. (2007). *Forces for Good: The Six Practices of High-Impact Nonprofits.* San Francisco, CA: Jossey-Bass.

Dees, J.G. (rev. 2001). *The Meaning of "Social Entrepreneurship."* Duke University Case Study. Retrieved July 25, 2011, from http://www.caseatduke.org/documents/dees_sedef.pdf.

DePree, M. (1990). *Leadership is an Art.* New York: Dell.

Goleman, D. (March-April 2000). **Leadership That Gets Results.** *Harvard Business Review.* Retrieved July 25, 2011, from http://www.hbr.org/2000/03/leadership-that-gets-results/ar/1.

Goleman, D. (November-December 1998). **What Makes A Leader?** *Harvard Business Review.* Retrieved July 25, 2011, from http://www.hbr.org/2004/01/what-makes-a-leader/ar/1.

Hoskins L. & Angelica, E.. *The Fieldstone Nonprofit Guide to Forming Alliances* (http://www.fieldstonealliance.org) Retrieved July 25, 11, from http://www.grantspace.org.

Light, P. (2002). **Grasping for the Ring: Defining Strong Nonprofit Leadership.** *CAN ALERT: The Journal for Nonprofit Managers, Volume 16, Number 4.*

Lipman-Blumen, J. (2000). *Connective Leadership: Managing in a Changing World.* Oxford: Oxford University Press.

MacMillan, I.C. & Thompson, J.D. (September 2010). **Making Social Ventures Work.** *Harvard Business Review.* Retrieved July 25, 2011, from http://www.hbr.org/2010/09/making-social-ventures-work/ar/1.

Martin, R.L. & Osberg, S. (Spring 2007). **Social Entrepreneurship: The Case for Definition.** *Stanford Social Innovation Review.* Retrieved July 25, 2011, from http://www.ssireview.org/images/articles/2007SP_feature_martinosberg.pdf.

Moreau, W. (1991). *Charging a Just Fee: A Guidebook for Nonprofit Organizations.* (Out of print. ISBN: 978-9991274096).

National Council of Nonprofits. *Capacity Building.* Retrieved July 25, 2011, from https://www.councilofnonprofits.org/capacity-building.

Oregon Public Broadcasting. (2005). *What is Social Entrepreneurship?* Bill Drayton quote retrieved July 25, 2011, from http://www.pbs.org/opb/thenewheroes/whatis/.

TCC Group and the Weingart Foundation. (2010). *Fortifying L.A.'s Nonprofit Organizations: Capacity-Building Needs and Services in Los Angeles County.* Retrieved July 25, 2011, from http://images. wireware.net/weingartfndorg/c_img/Weingart%20Report_Final.pdf.

Thompson, J.L. (2002). *The World of the Social Entrepreneur, The International Journal of Public Sector Management.*

Wertheimer, M. (2007). *The Board Chair Handbook, Second Edition.* Washington, DC: BoardSource.

CHAPTER 2: LEGAL

American Bar Association. (2003). *Guidebook for Directors of Nonprofit Corporations, Second Edition.* Chicago: American Bar Association.

Holmgren, N. (1997). *10 minutes to better board meetings.* New York: Planned Parenthood Federation of America.

Moreau, W. (1991). *Charging a Just Fee - A Guidebook for Nonprofit Organizations.* Community Council of Greater Dallas.

State of California Franchise Tax Board. (2010). *Exempt Organizations – Filing Requirements and Filing Fees.* Retrieved July 25, 2011, from http://www.ftb.ca.gov/forms/misc/1068.pdf.

State of California Franchise Tax Board. (2010). *Forms and Instructions 3500: 2010 Exemption Application Booklet.* Retrieved July 25, 2011, from http://www.ftb.ca.gov/forms/misc/3500bk.pdf.

State of California, Office of the Secretary of State. (2010). *Organization of California Nonprofit, Nonstock Corporations.* Retrieved July 25, 2011, from http://www.sos.ca.gov/business/corp/ pdf/articles/corp_artsnp.pdf.

United States Department of the Treasury – Internal Revenue Service. (2011). *Tax Information for Charities & Other Non-Profits.* Retrieved July 25, 2011, from http://www.irs.gov/charities/index. html?navmenu=menu1.

CHAPTER 3: BOARDS AND GOVERNANCE

BoardSource. (2011). *Assessing Your Performance.* Retrieved July 25, 2011, from http://www.boardsource.org/Spotlight.asp?ID=14.530.

BoardSource. (2011). *What are the legal responsibilities of nonprofit boards?* Retrieved July 25, 2011, from http://www.boardsource.org/Knowledge.asp?ID=3.364.

BoardSource. (2011). *What control does a nonprofit founder have over the organization?* Retrieved July 25, 2011, from http://www.boardsource.org/Knowledge.asp?ID=3.200.

BoardSource. (2003). *The Nonprofit Board's Guide to Bylaws.* Washington, DC: BoardSource.

CompassPoint. (1999). **Should Boards Have Committees, and if so, Which Ones?** *Board Café, Vol. 3, No. 1.* Retrieved July 25, 2011, from http://www.compasspoint.org/should-boards-have-committees-and-if-so-which-ones.

Fisman, R., Khurana, R. & Martenson, E. (Summer 2009). **Mission-Driven Governance.** *Stanford Social Innovation Review.*

Governance Matters. (2011). *Good Governance Guide.* Retrieved July 25, 2011, from http://www.governancematters.org/index.cfm?organization_id=56&section_id=1086

Herman R.D. & Associates. (2004). *The Jossey-Bass Handbook of Nonprofit Leadership and Management, Second Edition.* San Francisco, CA: Jossey-Bass.

Hopkins, B. (2009). *Legal Responsibilities of Nonprofit Boards, Second Edition.* Washington, DC: BoardSource.

Ingram, R.T. (2009). *Ten Basic Responsibilities of Nonprofit Boards, Second Edition.* Washington, DC: BoardSource.

Kern, D. (2011). *The Role of the Nonprofit Board Chair.* Posted to http://new.org/blog/?p=729.

Klein, K. (2000). **How to Get Your Board to Raise Money: Plan X.** *Grassroots Fundraising Journal.* Retrieved July 25, 2011, from http://www.grassrootsfundraising.org/mm5/merchant.mvc?Screen=PROD&Store_Code=G&Product_Code=v19_n2_art01-DLD.pdf.

Klein, K. (2000). **The Board and Fundraising.** *Grassroots Fundraising Journal.* Retrieved July 25, 2011, from http://www.grassrootsfundraising.org/magazine/bod_boardandfr.html.

McNamara, C. *Typical Types of Board Committees.* Free Management Library. Retrieved July 25, 2011, from http://www.managementhelp.org/boards/brdcmtte.htm.

Perry, G. (2007). *Fired Up Fundraising: Turn Board Passion into Action.* Hoboken, NJ: John Wiley & Sons, Inc.

Wertheimer, M. (2007). *The Board Chair Handbook, Second Edition.* Washington, DC: BoardSource.

CHAPTER 4: FINANCE

Financial Accounting Standards Board. (2008). *Statement of Financial Accounting Standards No. 116: Accounting for Contributions Received and Contributions Made.* Retrieved from http://www.fasb.org/pdf/aop_FAS116.pdf.

Financial Accounting Standards Board. (2010). *Statement of Financial Accounting Standards No. 117: Financial Statements of Not-for-Profit Organizations.* Retrieved from http://www.fasb.org/pdf/aop_FAS117.pdf.

Kaye, J. & Masaoka, J. (1993). *Finance Manual.* Washington, D.C.: National Minority AIDS Council.

CHAPTER 5: FUNDRAISING

Giving USA Foundation. (2011). *Giving USA 2011: Executive Summary.* Retrieved from http://www.givingusareports.org/free.php.

The Nonprofit Research Collaborative. (2010). *November 2010 Fundraising Survey.* Retrieved July 25, 2011, from http://www2.guidestar.org/rxg/news/publications/nonprofits-and-economy-october-2010.aspx.

Wing, K., Roeger, K.L. & Pollak, T.H. (2010). *The Nonprofit Sector in Brief: Public Charities, Giving and Volunteering, 2010.* Washington, DC: Urban Institute.

CHAPTER 6: MARKETING AND COMMUNICATIONS

Cause Communications. (2005). *Communications Toolkit.* Retrieved July 25, 2011, from http://www.causecommunications.org/resources.php.

CHAPTER 7: STRATEGIC PLANNING

La Piana, D. (2008). *The Nonprofit Strategy Revolution: Real-Time Strategic Planning in a Rapid-Response World.* Saint Paul, MN: Fieldstone Alliance.

McNamara, C. (2007). *Field Guide to Nonprofit Strategic Planning and Facilitation.* Minneapolis: Authenticity Consulting.

CHAPTER 8: EVALUATION

Colorado Nonprofit Association. *FAQs & Resources: Evaluation.* Retrieved July 25, 2011, from https://www.coloradononprofits.org/EvaluationFAQs.cfm#Pilot.

Joint Committee on Standards for Educational Evaluation. *Program Evaluation Standards Statements.* Retrieved August 26, 2011, from http://www.jcsee.org/program-evaluation-standards/program-evaluation-standards-statements.

USDA Food & Nutrition Service. (2005). *Nutrition Education: Principles of Sound Impact Evaluation.* Retrieved July 25, 2011, from http://www.fns.usda.gov/oane/menu/Published/NutritionEducation/Files/EvaluationPrinciples.pdf.

W.K. Kellogg Foundation. (2004). *Logic Model Development Guide.* Battle Creek, MI: W.K. Kellogg Foundation.

CHAPTER 10: TECHNOLOGY AND FACILITIES

Aaker, J. & Smith, A. (2011). **The Dragonfly Effect.** *Stanford Social Innovation Review.* Retrieved July 25, 2011, from http://www.ssireview.org/articles/entry/the_dragonfly_effect/.

Bennett, S. (2005). *The Accidental Techie.* Saint Paul, MN: Fieldstone Alliance.

Chan, E. (2006). *How Technology is Funded: The Basics.* Posted to http://www.techsoup.org/learningcenter/funding/page4808.cfm.

CommonCraft. (2008). *Social Media in Plain English.* Retrieved July 25, 2011, from http://commoncraft.com/socialmedia.

Idealware. (2011). *A few good... series.* Retrieved July 25, 2011, from http://www.idealware.org/ (search "a few good").

Idealware. (2011). *The Technology Pyramid.* Retrieved July 25, 2011, from https://salsa.democracyinaction.org/o/957/p/salsa/event/common/public/?event_KEY=66234.

Livingston, G. (2011). *4 Social Trends Impacting the Future of Online Fundraising.* Posted to http://www.mashable.com/2011/01/27/social-fundraising-trends/.